HARK

Also by Alice Vincent

Why Women Grow: Stories of Soil, Sisterhood and Survival

Rootbound: Rewilding a Life

HARK

HOW WOMEN LISTEN

Alice Vincent

CANONGATE

First published in Great Britain in 2025
by Canongate Books Ltd, 14 High Street, Edinburgh EH1 1TE

canongate.co.uk

1

Copyright © Alice Vincent, 2025

The right of Alice Vincent to be identified as the
author of this work has been asserted by her in accordance
with the Copyright, Designs and Patents Act 1988

No part of this book may be used or reproduced in any manner for
the purpose of training artificial intelligence technologies or systems.
This work is reserved from text and data mining (Article 4(3)
Directive (EU) 2019/790).

British Library Cataloguing-in-Publication Data
A catalogue record for this book is available on
request from the British Library

ISBN 978 1 80530 206 3

Typeset in Bembo STD by Palimpsest Book Production Ltd,
Falkirk, Stirlingshire

Printed and bound by CPI Group (UK) Ltd, Croydon CR0 4YY

The manufacturer's authorised representative in the EU for product
safety is Authorised Rep Compliance Ltd, 71 Lower Baggot Street,
Dublin D02 P593 Ireland
(arccompliance.com)

CONTENTS

PREFACE	*1*
Autumn Equinox	5
DISCORD	8
Spring Equinox, 8 p.m.	23
The Second Day of Spring, 4 a.m.	26
QUIETENING	29
The Second Day of Spring, 5.22 a.m.	43
HOME SOUNDS	45
The Third Day of Spring	55
INNER VOICE	58
MISOPHONIA	69
The Last Day in May	82

GHOSTS	88
DEEP LISTENING	99
WHITE NOISE	109
July	117
VIBRATIONS	124
ECHOES	147
Autumn	162
MIRRORS	168
WHISPERS	178
February	190
PHONE LINES	194
TRANSLATION	210
BRIDGES	226
Late Winter	237
DELPHI	241
ERAS	257
FRITH	266
EVOLUTION	273
DUSK	284
The Last Sunday in May	292
FURTHER READING	297
ACKNOWLEDGEMENTS	301

For Corin

'I hear thunder, I hear thunder / hark, don't you?'

PREFACE

I was small when I first saw a tuning fork. My father took it in his hand and struck it on his thigh before placing it on a wooden table. I remember the high, ghostly note ringing out, something that sounded almost impossible. Something conjured.

It sounded almost impossible because to my small, clumsy, childish hands it was, physically, impossible. My siblings and I messed around with the tuning fork, putting it on different parts of our bodies to feel our bones vibrate. But I didn't have the dexterity or the strength to make it ring. The fork, we were told, was brittle and somewhat precious; I might break it.

You can see a tuning fork vibrate as you hear its song. Get close enough, and you can feel the tiny movements in the air between the tines. The sound is something that exists because it is created in that moment, an energy that existed in a different form just seconds before.

The fork belonged to my mother; she used it to tune the guitar that gathered dust in the study and it was kept in the desk there. A docile, immobile object that could be sparked into life and used as a barometer. The thing that could set all of the other instruments into alignment. One small piece of metal too complicated and deceptively simple for me to operate.

There was a time in my life when sound felt like it was everything to me because it moved my body and it smoothed my brain and elevated my being into higher planes. Then there was a time in my life when I felt almost divorced from sound. As a hearing woman, sound has defined how I live; it shapes what brings me joy and where I spend my time, it changes the functions of my brain and my body. As a girl, I was taught that we grew up to become good listeners: that women socialised by talking to one another in a way that men did not. My ability to do this was as much a part of my learned womanhood as knowing how to apply make-up or think about the shape of my body.

Learning how to become a woman was noisy. The teen magazines with the shouty cover lines and the gossip rags with their circles of shame; the endless lists of things we should be and do and wear and say, a rampant cacophony of criticism and confines disguised as advice. From these fledgling years we emerged into a society where defending one another from the hands of older men was as much a part of the nightclub landscape as listening to the music we went there to dance to. In work, in dating, as we navigated our social and inner lives, there was noise. Then we grew up, perhaps we settled down, maybe we had children. The soundtrack changed; not quieter, just different.

Who was setting the tuning fork for all this noise? Sound holds power, just as money and the privilege of hearing ability does. Sound shapes my life, as it does for many of us. When I think about what it is to be a hearing woman living among it all, I wonder what I'm listening to without realising it – and I wonder what I am not hearing.

We only know our own experience of listening. As with our other senses, it is impossible to entirely know how others see or smell or hear, even if we love them, even if we have made them with our own bodies. We will never know what the world looks or sounds like to another person. But I still wanted to find out. Being a woman was noisy, but perhaps if we learned how to listen to our sisters, to attune to how life sounded for them, we could find meaning. There are ways of living that exist like the note of a tuning fork: inert until they are jolted into action, when they appear as an energy we didn't recognise before and reverberate with it. Maybe we will find our bodies resonating in ways that are more honest and revelatory and transcendent than those we had been taught. We could give voice to the things that we didn't think anybody else could hear, or open ourselves up to new things entirely. With them, we could make new spaces in which to be.

Sound, I thought, can do that. Sound is there. It just needs to be tuned into.

Autumn Equinox

There's an unspoken competition in the maternity assessment unit, and the women who are most visibly pregnant win. We are early and as I sit on the plastic benches waiting to be called in, I watch them arrive through the lift doors, these women, swollen and slow. It seems impossible and inevitable that I will become one of them. Months later, when my ribcage has opened to accommodate the swell of my stomach, I will sit back and watch the excited and nervous women walk through the lift doors and feel a strange mixture of nostalgia and superiority. But that is a long way off yet.

My husband Matt and I are here because there is something growing inside me. Not a baby, not yet. A collection of cells and tissue, no bigger than a plum. A secret I have become bored of keeping. A change of state that will change our lives. We are here to have it examined through my skin, through cold jelly, through wires and screens. We are here to listen to its heartbeat.

A large part of me still can't entirely believe it. I deliberated over whether or not to have a child for years, and now we are on the cusp of parenthood. It has not otherwise made itself known, aside from making me uncomfortable at night, and so I have tussled with the enormous non-existence of it. Later, I will tell people I can't know how my life will be after the baby is born but, inwardly, I know this is an acceptable half-truth: I am resolute; I will not let them define me, I will continue to write and work and drink a little and swim in cold water, just as I will up until the day they are born. I will not lose my sense of self. I will not become one of those women who fritters away conversation on matters of milk and nap schedules. I will not go to soft play on the weekends. I will manage, I will cope, it will not be as bad as they all make out.

That is all to come. For now, I must have my blood taken and lift up my feet so I do not faint and have a glass of water and lie down on the table and feel affronted as the waistband of my underwear is pushed down and jelly is smeared all over my gently bulging stomach. The room is busy; this is a teaching faculty and students appear to take turns in trying to find the foetus. The wand is pushed firmly against the skin between my hips. The screen above us flashes through incomprehensible shades of grey. The room is stiff with quiet. The medics, all puttering around behind my prone body, speak in codified riddles. My husband and I make eye contact, waiting for the sight that will change our lives. We are not sure yet if everything is okay, and I can feel the panic begin to build in my veins. After some time, the man holding the transducer to my stomach says, 'Well, that's one baby!' before watching for our reaction, as if joking about having twins is something he does to every newly pregnant person who walks through the door. We sag with relief, let out stifled little laughs. We have seen nothing, we have only this to go on. But then we hear it: a rapid, pulsing whoosh of white noise. An undeniable rhythm, the strange bones of a song I have made inside me. Our child's heartbeat.

I am struck by how much it reminds me of water, as if I am a ship upon a sea, looking out for dangers. These dark and undefinable depths. It is fast and it is strong and it is ours, ours, ours, this tiny organ that signals the baby's aliveness. It is astonishing to me. And it is soon over: the medics must get on with their measurements, the heartbeat noise is muted. In its absence, a sinking quiet and a silent roar rush in. These are the sounds of our lives changing.

DISCORD

In the days after the first scan, I kept thinking about it – the fierce wet rush of the heart beating inside me. I couldn't wholly make sense of it belonging to a person, so I thought about it as noise; how fast it was, how loud, how we could only hear it through wires and machines, how easily they could be switched on and off.

I'd been thinking about sound for a while, too. It started before the pregnancy, that strange new state of being I was trying to understand; possibly even years ago, on the pale drying grass of a festival tent floor. Perhaps that was when I first realised – first admitted to myself – that sound had changed for me. That I'd lost my grip on it.

I was a musical child who grew into a music-obsessed adolescent. I made music my work and my identity, only for it to gradually vanish from my life and my brain. I barely listen to music now, and I haven't meaningfully for years. In its absence, I had become a person who lived with the whistles and thuds of tinnitus as a backing track, overwhelmed by the choice of things to listen to that are available at our fingertips – podcasts and videos and albums and songs and mixtapes and meditations. There was a while when I was very knowledgeable about certain kinds of music, where I would wear rare band T-shirts and take pride in owning certain CDs. I bought into the commodification of the culture because it gave me an identity to cling on to. But that seemed beyond my reach now. I felt as if I were cast adrift in a sea of sound that other people knew how to navigate. Unlike them, I existed quietly in the sounds of life. If I engaged with those sounds, I wondered if I might be able to find out why and how they became so hollow. Part of me longed for the excitement I used to feel when I listened to music as a younger woman; part of me wanted to find her. Beyond music, I wondered where properly engaging with sound might take me. I wanted to know what I would find out – both in the world and about myself – if I followed sound into new corners of listening.

Before the baby started to grow in my body, I whispered a request up and out into high blue desert skies: 'I want to know what this sound can do.' I was standing beneath a porthole in the middle of a dome made of wood. I was in the Integratron, a round, two-storey building located off a lonely windswept road in the Mojave Desert. I wondered if I would come out a different kind of person.

I had been wanting to come here for five years, ever since I discovered it was the source of extraordinary sound baths. At that point I was still defining myself by my relationship to music – as someone who wrote about it for the newspaper I worked for; as someone who went clubbing and to raves in warehouses; someone who could set the measure of a pop star's performance into 450 neat little words and a few tiny stars. Since then, I had become quietly hooked on the deep relaxation sound baths provided, a bodily connecting with sound that I was increasingly struggling to find elsewhere. But by the time I had finally reached the Integratron – written my name on a chalkboard; sugar-paper ticket for a sound bath in my hand – I was conscious of something I had suspected but not wanted to confront: that the relationship I held with sound and music, something that used to ground my life, was withering. That it had all but disappeared and had done so almost by stealth. Part of me thought I might find some resonance here, in this wooden dome across an ocean and a continent from my home, that I could hold on to. I was hoping to hear something – some internal insight or long-lost spark of connection – that could help me to listen more deeply.

I had dedicated my youth to making music part of my life because it made sense when so little else did. I used it as an escape and as a source of meaning. I was a girl so uncomfortable with herself she could barely look in the mirror, but music gave me a costume I could make my own. The silly, thrashy rebellion of early Noughties pop punk allowed me to dream myself out of the cul-de-sacs of my village upbringing into a world of skateparks and school proms. The abstract, twanging guitars and lackadaisical vocals of indie arrived with my adolescence and offered another, larger world, one where ideas and books and artists were thrown around as keys to understanding. Jeff Buckley for heartbreak, Giant Drag for driving, Yeah Yeah Yeahs for freewheeling feelings, the Libertines and Basement Jaxx for dancing. I fell so deeply for music because the sound of it offered my confused, changing body a way of feeling and a compass for what it was to grow up. It gave me a means of understanding the pulsing, messy matter of life I didn't otherwise have the language for.

For a while I was good at speaking that language. Good enough to turn it into words on a page and pay my bills with them. In the process, though, my connection with music changed and shrank. The once-satisfying thud of a syncopated drumbeat became a distant soundtrack. The eerie caterwaul of an avant-garde vocalist faded into unknowable upper registers. By the time I was pregnant, I felt clumsy when speaking about music. The details felt small and removed, something for other people – other people who cared more, who carved out more time for it, who felt more for it. It felt too unwieldy a thing for me to carry when there was so much else to think about. I was at another point of transition: my body was changing faster than I realised; inside it another body was growing fingernails and cartilage and blood. Once again, I was grasping at something to help me make sense of it.

I am non-disabled and hearing: I do not define as d/Deaf or hard-of-hearing. Music's absence in my life wasn't due to a physical inability to listen so much as it was caused by a gulf I hadn't asked for. I had lived different kinds of lives, and I was working out what to take with me and what to leave behind.

Perhaps this was just what it was to get older. When I had been that teenager, I asked my mum how she never got into the Smiths; she was around in the Eighties, she could have seen them play while they were still together. She replied, wearily, that she was raising children. The music I've inherited from her, the stuff she raised us on and which I still find great comfort in, it all dates from her own girlhood. Elton John, James Taylor, Sandy Denny, Joni Mitchell, Simon & Garfunkel. She would sing David Bowie's 'Space Oddity' to us as a lullaby.

That trip to the Integratron, to the desert, took place at a time when life was both heightened and on pause. Our wedding had taken place days earlier and we were travelling through America on our honeymoon. Everything was glossy and bright, a few weeks of adventure and indulgence before we returned to our home as husband and wife. Caught between ocean roads and sprawling highways, we were held in this moment of change: we had committed to one another for life, we just didn't know what that looked like yet. I was driving away from something and towards something else.

•

The Integratron is an extraordinary sound chamber because it is made almost entirely out of wood – the only one in America to be so – and said to be acoustically perfect. You can see the neat little dots where dowels have been meticulously hammered in. The end result is a building that is akin to an enormous cello; to stand inside it is to be cocooned. We were invited to stand in the middle of the round room, beneath the plug, where sunlight falls through its window and warms the floorboards beneath. The sound waves move differently here: back and forth around the curved walls, and up and down through its core. I whispered my request and almost immediately heard my voice echoed back at me, polyphonically fragmented into layers of sound. It was as if I had become a microphone of myself.

I was following thousands of other people in standing inside the Integratron and whispering something. The three sisters who now own and run it as a family business first went there in the mid-Eighties and have since hosted all manner of visitors, from Tibetan monks and army veterans with PTSD to influencers and astronomers. Most arrive seeking something from sound, and I was among them.

We settled down on thick mats laid beneath the domed ceiling. A woman named Christine moved batons around the inside of bowls made of crystal. I had been in sound and gong baths before – in tents at festivals, in yoga studios in South London suburbs – but I had never seen someone play the instruments; normally participants are encouraged to lie down and close their eyes before the sound begins. Christine got far closer to the bowls than I had anticipated, almost as if they were part of her. Before she began, she explained that each of the bowls would affect a different part of our bodies, and I felt the sound move through mine: deep vibrations in my feet and hands, in my hips and stomach. By the time it hit my solar plexus, I was in a state of pliable semi-conscious relaxation, neither awake nor asleep, both present and absent.

I had never experienced sound like this before, as if it were played from deep inside my head, rather than being channelled through my ears. Not on headphones, not through a speaker stack. It plummeted further inwards than the intimacy of a whisper and it felt louder than a shout. The sounds were played from crystal bowls but they reminded me of many other things, from a cry or a howl to the electronic patterns of a siren or house music. Over and over, I felt my mind drift as these frequencies vibrated through my body. At some point, after about 45 minutes or so, I was brought back around to consciousness: I saw the searing blue of the sky through the window above my head, I felt my cheeks tighten in a gentle smile. I was dozy and blissed out on the resonance of a supercharged nap. But I had also awoken to feel something brand new.

•

At times it felt like I was travelling on a sound wave, oscillating between the past I thought I was sure of and a future I could not predict. I wanted a child, but I was wary of what one might do to my life. Much of my young adulthood had been defined by my relationship to music; now I was a woman in her mid-thirties about to have a baby and felt defined by music's absence. I was neither old nor young; I felt increasingly small even as my body took up more space with every passing month. Men could become fathers without their bodies changing, while society rendered mothers and mothering invisible and infantile. I couldn't yet see – or hear – what other, truer versions of it existed.

I was aware I was moving between one state and another. Commuting, from a womb that emptied every month to one that was swelling by the day. From an adult life I knew the parameters and freedoms of into one that, I was told, was riddled with grim surprise and entrapment. Everyone seemed excited about the fact a baby was coming, but only a handful of people told me why parenthood might be a worthwhile experience.

The sounds of my life – the air traffic over my garden or the trundling of the road outside, the calls of the neighbours, the voice notes my friends and I exchanged – weren't silent so much as a strange and clanging cacophony. Among these, the noises inside my body: a wariness over a future that didn't seem to fit the expectations I'd ever held for myself, the yawning grief of a life I had lost before I was ready to lose it. I wanted to smooth these discordant notes out, plot them on a staff, feel like I could play again – not on any specific instrument so much as in my life more broadly. If I could find new ways of listening, perhaps I could understand better who I was. If I could listen more deeply, I might be able to make those crucial connections: between what I was then and who I was becoming, between the life I felt removed from and the one I was yet to know. If I could listen deeply enough, I reasoned, the sounds of my life could once again offer me an education in feeling. Listening could offer a more connected way of being.

Onto this strange soundscape the advice and expectations landed. In being pregnant I was suddenly a repository for information I'd never asked for. I was given warnings and threats under the guise of advice: I would not read once I had the baby, I was told. I would not write. I would not sleep, nor have time to myself. I would not leave the house, not without taking an hour to prepare for it. Before my stomach was bulging enough to even be visible to the outside world, people called me 'mama'. I was told what to eat (tablespoons of salmon roe, for good brain growth), what to do and what not to do. I was advised to spend money I don't have, to freeze the blood of my umbilical cord, in case my child became so ill in later life they needed to access their stem cells. I was told what to read and what to 'make the most of'. When to rest and when to exercise. What to wear and what to buy and which groups to join and what won't matter and what will; what the baby will need and what they won't. Rarely was I asked my opinion, which was just as well, as often I didn't know. It was all so loud in my head.

Sometimes I still wrote about music, a loose tether to this old self. While I had left the newspaper where I had made it my work, I'd been writing gig reviews and features about pop stars for over a decade, and occasionally I'd crop up in the mind of a commissioning editor.

I relished and regretted these sporadic reviews in equal measure. On some level they offered a chance to connect with a diminishing part of my life, the flickering ghost of the girl I used to be. On another they reinforced the fact that I was no longer her. I told myself it was good to flex old muscles, to push myself into new spaces, to participate with the realm of music that was becoming ever more unfamiliar to me. And so, I prepared for these shows like an out-of-practice athlete, limbering up by listening to an artist's back catalogue and finding out what I could about them, turning up to see if I could still run the race. Part of me hoped each time that this would be the gig to change everything, that this would be the performance, the show, the song that reignited my love of music, that unlocked whatever was closed and allowed it all to come streaming back in.

The muscle memory hadn't faded. I stuck to the same routine: stand alone in the guest-list queue outside the backstage door of a venue — it now felt stranger to me to review a gig with company than go to one by myself — ten minutes before the set time, working my brain into familiar grooves. Take in the crowd, the atmosphere, the backing band. Ferret out a spot on the mezzanine if the main floor was chaotic, or stand among the couples on a night out if the upper levels were too rammed. I knew how to do this: how to get onto the Tube while everyone else was still leaving the venue, rattle out a review into my notes app, file 450 words that captured 90 minutes of live music by dawn, then largely forget it happened. Words, music: the two things I'd spent years trying to combine had become one slick, soulless machine.

•

I am at the exact midpoint of my pregnancy when I push against the tide of commuters to review a gig in town. I'm retracing old steps, curious as to whether I can layer up different parts of my life through geography alone. Part of the reason I took this review on is because of its location: two decades ago, I made a teenage pilgrimage here to see my first gig in the city. Now, a gleaming new entertainment complex has been built on top of it. I grew up in the countryside, an hour away on the train. London was close enough to make adolescent pilgrimages but it was — and is — a big, filthy, place; one that demands you keep your wits about you. We were still teenagers when we first came to the Astoria, a 1920s warehouse-turned-theatre where certain chunks of pop and rock history were made. That night, the Polyphonic Spree were playing: a 24-strong, robe-clad choir from Texas who sing optimistic indie pop inspired by the 1960s. It was hardly dangerous, but it felt wild; to be out in London, staring up at a stage, the sweat and smoke and presence of thousands of adults standing behind us. Each night, I fell asleep staring at the crowd from this stage — I'd stuck a poster of the Libertines playing the Astoria across from my bed. Now I was standing in the pit, singing. The band swayed in their colourful robes, incanting harmonies about the sun, and while I was unconvinced by the hippy overtones I felt my body buzz with the sheer reverberance of it. Music, I realised, existed to be seen and felt live. I would spend years chasing that feeling.

Five years later, the Astoria was pulled down. The McDonald's where we ate chicken nuggets before the show still stands, glowing on the corner of Tottenham Court Road, but the rest of the area is so different it is dislocating to stand there. For nearly all the time I've lived in London this part of town has been a building site, cleared and boarded off while works happened in the tunnels below ground. At some point after lockdown, I emerged from the Tube and found a corner of the city I'd never seen before. Searing walls of glinting bronze and shimmering screens filled with advertisements for Netflix shows beamed down on the pavement. This was, I later learned, the Outernet. To inhabit it feels dystopian: a collection of large, partially open-air boxes smothered in video screens blaring out graphics. I stand on the margins and watched people walk in, sit on the boxy little benches beneath a sea of logos and take photos on their phones.

    The artist I have been sent here to review is a former wedding singer who found fame after posting videos to TikTok. At the time of his gig, he has nearly 24 million followers. I watch him rattle through a 45-minute set of forgettable songs constructed from the pulse points of modern pop: millennial whoops, power-ballad choruses, breakbeat rhythms. Between him leaving the stage and returning for the encore, two QR codes appear on the full-bleed screens he'd stood in front of. We are urged to scan them; they take us to a website to buy his album. I give him three stars.

    When I'd stood on that same patch of land as a teenager, I felt like I had discovered something that would shape my life. Twenty years later the same place has left me bored and numb. I long for something. I don't want to return – the effervescent capacity for music I fed as a teenager was something born of adolescent energy and naivety – but I do want to feel moved by sound. I want to plumb further into the reaches of what noise can do to our bodies and minds. Our lives are built of sound and rhythm; sometimes this is turned into what is recognised as music, more often it becomes a backdrop to our living. This is what I want to grasp, to take hold of and nestle in. I want to understand why sound can make our skin prick or our minds wander, how it resonates within us or makes us angry; I want to understand why the brief, rapid whoosh of an ultrasound can make us cry. In a world where the stuff of what we create becomes content, I am hungry for meaning. If I keep seeking out resonance, I think, eventually something might connect.

When I was younger, music held freedom. Now my future feels like a series of traps: ones formed by the cost of childcare and life inside a postpartum body; more broadly, a life in a body that the world seems increasingly punitive towards as right-wing governments crack down on reproductive rights. If I can find music again, perhaps I can inhabit the freedoms of my youth – or a version of them. I long to embody the same relief that came from shaking my limbs out on a dance floor; the softly physical recognition that arrived when a lyric aligned with your own experience.

As the seasons change and my body with them it becomes easier to find ways to take up space, to forge an identity on terms I can understand. Quietly, I push myself against the noise. I am fortunate: aside from the tiredness, I have few other pregnancy symptoms. I continue to ride my bike to work – as my stomach swells, I find it easier to push pedals than walk. From the saddle I tune into the sounds I have learned from the past 15 years of cycling in cities: the rumble of an approaching van, the purr of a black cab, the warning signal of a heavy goods vehicle turning left. I zip myself into neoprene and plunge my body into cold water in the depths of winter, feeling my toes grow numb as there is snow on the ground; I listen to the slug and gush of it against the walls of the lido, the sound of my breath turning into steam as it leaves my mouth.

When I am eight months pregnant, I go to a club with a friend to watch a band who are having their own resurgence, 20 years after they hit the charts as teenagers. We sing and dance, the lyrics and dance movements etched into our bodies in ways we didn't realise were still there. For a rare, fleeting moment, my body is two things at once: a girl repeating these earworms in a shopping centre with her friends, a woman growing a baby, its feet kicking to the beat. Everything is on its axis, but it feels like reclamation.

Spring Equinox, 8 p.m.

I AM IN A LARGE POOL, in the middle of a room that's trying to mask its pragmatism with a thin veil of comfort; there is a lot of moulded purple plastic and dozens of plug sockets. There are outlets for oxygen. The floors are easy to bleach. The double bed folds up into the wall, in case one on wheels needs to be brought in. This is something I will learn later.

For now, it is just the pool, the water and the hiss of the gas and air. The lights are low. Around the corner, almost out of sight, a midwife sits at a glowing screen. I am left largely alone. This is work that, for the most part, only I can do. My body has been taking over for 16 hours now. Every few minutes, the muscles that hold another smaller, growing body contract. They do so with a pain that is so deep and strangely pure that it forces me to turn inward. I close my eyes; I breathe heavily. I concentrate on the pain, on its passage across my lower back and between my hips. I clumsily force a plastic mouthpiece between my teeth and huff on the invisible analgesic substances that are as strong as I'm allowed. It still hurts, of course it does.

Between contractions, a machine is wheeled over and snaked against my body. The midwife is checking the baby. I listen to the heartbeat and, every time, ask: 'Are they okay? Is it okay?' The midwife nods; a contraction flows in. I need reassurance to navigate these waters.

A lot of it is waiting. Waiting for another contraction, waiting for my cervix to dilate. Waiting for the next stage of labour to take place. Waiting for an examination. Waiting for the baby. My husband is constantly around, somewhere in the periphery, whispering encouragement and moving a paper fan through the air in my direction. It often sounds as if he is in another room or behind a pane of glass. So much of this is quieter than I had been led to believe.

I haven't made a birthing playlist. I expected the baby to be late, but I went into labour a day before they were due. The basket where the baby will sleep has not been unpacked. I still have emails to answer, tasks to do. When it is decided that we should put on music in the birthing room I request an album called *Titanic Rising* by Weyes Blood, an American musician a few months older than me whose records have soundtracked various moments of solitude in my life. Perhaps the music is meant to inspire oxytocin, the loved-up hormone that aids labour; perhaps it is meant to further disguise the fact this is all happening in hospital; perhaps it is meant to help pass the time. I imagine all three.

I choose *Titanic Rising* because it is the record I grasp for most. I enjoy the lush, cinematic string arrangements and the way that Natalie Laura Mering's — Weyes Blood's real name — voice floats atop them. It is music that carries me away a little. I don't expect it to mean anything.

Another contraction begins in a well I didn't know was in me and builds quickly, a dull rip through my consciousness. The see-sawing piano chords that open 'A Lot's Gonna Change' walk out of the iPhone speaker above a synth intro. I push my body further beneath the water's surface, resting my neck on one of the pool's little steps. Mering sings wistfully for a time before, when she was just a girl. The drumbeat kicks in. Wet hair slicks against my neck. Strings build. The nitrous oxide and oxygen have been bubbling for hours now and I'm softly high. The contraction reaches its apex; my lower body is racked and tense with agony. And I hear the chorus refrain, the one that repeats the title. A lot is going to change, it's changing right now. Mering sings of new beginnings, of falling trees and high tides and lying hearts. And I am left, temporarily empty of pain as the contraction leaves my body, still so full with danger and possibility, floating in this pool of water and sound.

The Second Day of Spring, 4 a.m.

TIME LOSES MEANING. My contractions grow stubborn, then absent themselves altogether. Something inexplicable has happened. The baby is close, close enough that the midwife can see the colour of their hair, but still somewhere else entirely. There was a window for me to push the baby out and it has passed. I agree to a change of plan and scene: we will go into theatre, anaesthetic will be injected into my spinal cord, I will be cut open and the baby will be pulled out.

We emerge out of the dim intimacy of the room with the pool into a corridor. I watch the fluorescent strip lights track my journey, clocking how many times I've seen this scene play out on screen, only now it is happening in my life. We head through the doors to the operating theatre and my senses are overloaded. The lights are scrutinising in their brightness; the theatre is filled with people talking, their blue scrubs rustling as they prepare for the surgery that will bring my child into the world. The air fills with a chorus of beeping machines, none of them harmonising, one in particular ringing out a three-note refrain in a strange, melancholy key. Through a high window the vestiges of the night recede. Dawn is on its way.

I lie on the table, numb from the ribs down, vaguely aware of all the people in the room. The drugs have vanished my pain and the strange, silent creature I have become starts to shrink. I crack jokes with the doctors; I see the fear in my husband's eyes; I catch a glimpse of the forceps, curved, massive and medieval, that will end my pregnancy. My surgery is the last in this team's shift. Magic FM, the radio station of twilight taxi drivers, fills the room. The pulsing guitar riff of ABBA's 'Waterloo' ripples out surreally.

Among it all I am searching for something else: the baby's heartbeat. For the past six months, it has been the only audible evidence of their existence, a liquid kind of white noise that managed to pull tears from my eyes when I first heard it, regular and rapid and miraculous. Since then, this rhythm inside of me has offered grounding, connection, release and relief. I may have become accustomed to the baby's movements — the angular persistence of their heel kicking beneath my ribs, the roll of their curved spine against my stretched skin — but hearing their heartbeat, an insistent whooshing, allowed me inside. It proved that they were real, a being of blood and beating life.

As both of us grew I heard it more often, became familiar with the blank fuzz of the machine reflecting the wet of my insides that transformed as the midwife pressed and found a baby. A repetition as innate and natural as a foaming wave against a rock.

The midwife has come with us to theatre, and straps round pads to my bloated stomach with Velcro belts. The monitor is almost within my reach; the midwife sits next to it, no longer in control of this space or this birth but another part of a puzzle that has become increasingly complex. She sees me watching it, searching for the only sound of the baby I have come to know. Silently, she understands and turns the monitor up. My ears tune into it, those recognisable beckoning waters of my child's blood, the surges and dips that mirror my own now-stilled contractions.

The anaesthetist, concentrating on something else, is baffled and irate, asks why the monitor is so loud. The midwife turns it down. Another medic says it was deafening; among the bleeping machinery that demarcates their working lives, it is an anomaly. But I feel I am straining for it, this sonic guarantee of my child's safe transition out of the water and into the air-breathing world. I suspect it could never really be loud enough.

QUIETENING

I HAVE SPENT WEEKS READING about anechoic chambers online and watching videos of people testing themselves to spend time in one. I mention it to a radio producer I know, and she tells me she lasted mere minutes, that she hated it and it frightened her. Those who know what an anechoic chamber is speak of them in the same hushed shudders as one might a potentially haunted building: as a place of uncanniness and discomfort, where strange things happen.

It takes me a while to get into one, but a few weeks before Christmas I am granted entry to the only acoustics laboratory in the city, and the only one willing to let me – someone who is not an academic, not a student of acoustics, not a client, simply someone who feels overwhelmed by noise – come in and sample the nothingness. I have been allocated an hour, which I had hoped to spend in the chamber, testing myself to see how much I could bear of air cushioned by foam. But the man who runs the laboratory is keen to tell me about its work. I get the sense that he revels in being an almost unseen force of power: the discoveries that are made here, in this squat, utilitarian little building with gaffa-taped floors and complicated-looking instruments, change how we experience the world, and yet, if this work is done well, it is completely invisible – we don't even notice it.

By the time we reach the chamber, I have been told many things and shown different experiments. Of the hour I have been given to spend here, there are 20 minutes left. I'm asked if I want the lights left on in the chamber or not – I'm among the half who would prefer it; the light switch is on the outside of the chamber. I'm asked if I can operate the door to get out, if I know to lift the long, heavy lever, and I show that I do. A research assistant asks how long I want to stay in and suggests 10 minutes. I say at least 15. Then they smile and pull the door to, and I am left in the chamber with this strange, still air. I let my voice out, sing a few bars. It sounds hollow and silly. I wonder if they can hear me, even though I know they can't. My hearing is still adjusting. I make some notes on paper, and when the scratch of my pen interrupts the silence, it feels like cheating. I bring my hands together in an underwhelming clap; it's a noise that sounds like a removal rather than a celebration.

After 12 minutes I become very conscious of the sounds

of my body. I swallow and hear liquid pushing down my throat. I am the first pregnant person to enter the chamber, and before I visit, I wonder if I will hear the sound of the additional water in my womb, the small tidal waves that connect us – me and the rapid, determined little heartbeat rising from the wet noises at the other end of the ultrasound wand. But most noticeable is the noise inside my own head; not an inner monologue but a soft, high-pitched ring and the repetitive whoosh of something – blood or air, perhaps? – inside my ear. I always thought that was the noise of being, it's a sound that's accompanied me for as long as I can remember, I've rarely noticed its absence. I suddenly feel tired in a novel, lumpen way, as if I have been concentrating very hard on something for several hours. In here, stripped of all noise outside of myself, I realise that I have been keying into my body without realising.

The door handle moves, and I blink at the person silhouetted against the brighter light beyond. It's the research assistant. He tells me I've been in for 18 minutes, it's time for me to leave – they need the chambers back for their students to use. I'm surprised and disappointed in equal measure. I didn't hear the baby's heartbeat. I haven't found the silence punishing or weird, but strangely meditative. I am newly conscious of the background noise that accompanies many of the hours I spend at home alone without music – working, or reading, or cooking – noise that I thought everyone heard but I now know to be unique to me, audible scars of the life I've lived, listening to music on headphones and dance floors. I can't work out if this is a sign that I've been listening better than I thought, that I've managed to make familiar the most intimate sounds of my daily existence, or a confirmation of my ambivalence to sound and music in my life.

 I thank the men and gather my things. I feel like I've failed, that I've come to seek quietude only to spend most of an hour listening to chatter. Even here, it has been hard to tune out the noise. The chamber has left me inexplicably heavy, as if I have spent the day travelling or woken up from a nap to find it dark outside. I push out of the laboratory and am besieged by noise. A pneumatic drill penetrates the road surface with a metallic whine, the wind pushes through the slick glass new-builds and whips past my ears, buses rumble by. I can no longer connect to the sounds inside my head. I leave a voice note on my phone and I feel like I am whispering. I knew I lived among a barrage of noise but this silence feels just as mystifying. I had anticipated the absence of sound to be quietly horrifying, to show me what I was missing, to be a kind of absence from which to start navigating a new way of listening, a new way of being. Instead, I was confronted with a comfort with silence I couldn't have imagined – and a familiarity with quietude I didn't realise I was living in.

•

I found the summer I fell pregnant unsettling. Twelve long weeks before any kind of certainty, bloated at night with nothing I could see and heavy in the day with a silent anxiety. The country was held firm in a heatwave and I withdrew from things – the news, the internet, staying more than a couple of hours when I saw my friends – in an attempt to make things feel less dizzying. I craved salt and water and edges, something that would make me feel small when what I was facing felt so big. I wanted to wade into the sea and let my body – so careering, so out of my control – float in the mass of something ancient and enormous.

I boarded a train to Cornwall and waited for a cab that never came before checking into a coastal path hotel that was trying to harness its fading grandeur. It was the beginning of August but the place still felt deserted somehow. Older couples sitting in armchairs before eating dinner in silence. I had thought that escaping London would provide me with the stillness that would ease the queasy restlessness inside, but when I arrived, I was deflated by how uncomfortable it all felt. I had left home because it felt claustrophobic; once I was away I stewed in homesickness. Part of my desire to leave the city for a few days was because I fetishised silence, something I'd imagined as the blissful nothingness that accompanies retreat; the peaceful tranquillity I'd encountered a few times in my life – while staying in a deserted Zen Buddhist monastery, up a Japanese mountain in the final days of winter; on the edge of a hiking trail, on a clear April day, in the highlands of southern Iceland. In my memory these were places where the atmosphere was so clear even sound didn't vibrate; a silence that would occasionally be punctured by a sign of life some minutes' distance away.

But I'd come somewhere silent – the hotel with its carpeted hallways and thick curtains, well-sealed windows and the eyrie-like little balcony looking out onto gardens – only to find it oppressive. I'd run away because I had told myself it was the last time I'd be able to: once the baby was here, I wouldn't be able to go away alone as easily. So far, my pregnancy had been almost ghostly, my state of change marked by a blue line on a piece of plastic and crushing fatigue. I thought about the fact I was growing a baby almost constantly, but it felt fantastical. I'd not realised that it was my body and its silent stowaway that was making me feel trapped.

A twelve-year-long silence passed between Kate Bush's seventh and eighth albums, during which time she removed herself from the public eye and the rampant album-release cycle that had defined her career for the previous 15 years. She had a baby and raised him, and the public didn't find out until he was 18 months old. Without any shows or songs to write about, the media compared her to Miss Havisham or Greta Garbo, outraged that she kept her life private. She spent six years recording *Aerial*, the album that emerged after her matrescence, which bore the cover of a waveform of blackbird song. On it is a song called 'Mrs Bartolozzi', in which Bush sings from the perspective of a woman who daydreams about wading into the sea while she's at home, doing laundry. Bush's spiralling vocals detail the kind of domestic drudgery people don't often write songs about; she splits apart the act of mopping and scrubbing, the different clothes that land in the laundry basket. She makes a whole, hopeful-sounding chorus just dedicated to the washing machine, with bold, silent pauses between the lyrics. Water, repetition, escape, domesticity. In a rare interview, Bush said that she was pleasantly surprised that listeners found the song funny, because she considered it 'one of the heaviest songs she'd ever written'.

My cravings for water and waves, sea and salt, were the only ones I experienced during my pregnancy. In the final wintry weeks of it I drove across the country, took trains before the dawn, to push my body into the water. In crossing the boundary between land and sea my own shifting state solidified: my body became something powerful rather than hampered. I would look back to land, which suddenly seemed so small and so far away, and realise that all I could hear was the water and the wind. A kind of comforting silence.

It took practice to get there. In Cornwall, during those first few weeks, I performed the other acts of holidaying: I walked the coastal path, I ate cooked breakfasts, I watched

TV from my enormous, borrowed bed. I was listless, I checked my phone too often. I barely spoke to anyone and the quiet felt crushing at times. Nobody apart from my husband knew that I was carrying what might become a baby; I was cut off and I was growing, silent among it all. The only thing that made sense was to walk down to the beach on the edge of the hotel grounds. Still, I was skittish around the water, my skin always takes take weeks to toughen up to the cold. I'd plunge in awkwardly, move my limbs too quickly to luxuriate, worry that my dry clothes would vanish before I made it back to shore. I preferred to sit on the shore afterwards, wrapped in a towel, feeling the salt crystallise on my skin. It never felt too quiet here.

I was four months pregnant when I entered the anechoic chamber. While I found the solitude of my time away claustrophobic, I was still hungry for silence. Since shedding the secrecy over my pregnancy, I had felt my relationship with sound and noise and music grow even more complicated. I was a reverberant mass of water and blood. I was ripening with uncertainty. Even the child in my womb no longer sat in silence. Increasingly, it felt that any quest to understand noise must begin with its absence. I wanted to experience silence: not respite, not hush, nor the tight, unspoken vacancy of a Tube carriage. Not the dull muffle that can be found in the countryside or even waking up on a snowy morning. But the deep, scientifically created silence of an anechoic chamber: a place where echo has been eliminated, so the only thing you are left with is still air, empty of vibration.

When the Second World War was declared in September 1939, author Virginia Woolf broke her habit of living between London and Sussex and instead settled into her country home, at Monk's House in the South Downs. She swapped a life of literary industry for one of slow domesticity, the noise of the city for rural quiet. While walking in January 1940 Woolf noted 'the silence, the pure disembodied silence'. As Harriet Baker points out in *Rural Hours: The Country Lives of Virginia Woolf, Sylvia Townsend Warner and Rosamond Lehman*, this retreat into external stillness reflected a shift Woolf was experiencing in her career and identity; her biography of Roger Fry had been published to no apparent recognition ('Complete silence surrounds that book' she wrote in her diary. 'It might have sailed into the blue and been lost') and in living away from the public eye in London she relished – and worried about – being 'no longer famous, no longer on a pedestal, no longer hawked in by societies'. Professionally, personally and literally, Woolf was caught in a state of in-between, an absence of noise that reflected a shift in who she thought she was.

Weeks passed. I tallied them on the app that showed me how the baby was growing inside me. Tentatively, I felt their body moving inside mine, a small whale breaching in unseen waters, two hands passing over one another in a washing up bowl. This was a silent thing, but the kicking began at the same point that the baby started to make sense of sound. I wondered what that must be like, to suddenly hear the heartbeat of the body that is carrying yours.

•

The anechoic chamber had made it impossible to ignore that I had tinnitus. The noises I'd always told myself were what quiet sounded like – a far-off, high-pitched ringing; a lower, persistent whump-whump-whump; sometimes a third, wavering sound that was almost like an alarm bell that somehow brought them together – were actually only heard by me, a dull layer of noise on top of everything else I ever heard. Quiet enough to be drowned out by a fan heater (approx. 50 decibels), but present enough to be exacerbated by other low-frequency noises, such as the gentle rhythm of the dishwasher or the ratcheting up of stress, which I always imagine to be the building whistle of a kettle boiling. It would worsen with a cold, transform into a deafening, muffling state not unlike being underwater. But I could usually distract myself from it in company or when I was among the other noise of the city. Nevertheless, in quiet spaces, which I increasingly occupied, it was there with me. It was there when I sat at my desk to work. In the deepest, stillest parts of the night, when I lay in bed and tried to sleep, it would sound far louder. Deep down, I suspect I was in denial about it: whatever noises I heard were not so imposing as to affect the decisions I made about life – I wasn't afraid of loud places, my movements weren't dictated by my hearing. Still, even 18 minutes in a soundproof room had been enough to show me that the bells and whistles of my existence were evidence that my hearing was probably damaged.

I thought of all the gigs I went to – dozens over my teenage years – when I would come home and lie in my childhood bed with my ears ringing, put a CD on low to try and wring the adrenaline out of my veins. The body I would often question when I was alone felt almost reshaped by the viscerality of standing in a sweaty, grimy room and watching music being made by older kids on a stage. I got hooked on those vibrations, wanted more of them, sought them out through the matted grass of festival fields and the gummy plastic of an earbud. I didn't tire of the excitement that came with walking through a club door and being physically confronted by noise – by the music, yes, but also the smell and the heat and the thick air of it, of other bodies moving and singing and stamping, of flesh and blood giving way to the invisible heft of sound waves. My addiction to music, to noise, to clubs, left me with ghosts of sounds that I could now hear even in the quietest places. All those notes and all those beats reduced to a strange chorus of whistling inside my head.

It had been a while since I had seen an audiologist, but there was a time in my life when I visited them quite frequently. The memories exist in my brain in fragments, like snippets of cine film. Sitting at a little table in a surgery wearing a pair of bulky headphones, a black tube with a red button on top. I'm told to press it when I hear a noise. There's a box of toys in the corner. I've been told this is a kind of game and I'll get a treat afterwards, but I know there's a significance to what I'm doing. The film putters out, and another one rolls: me turning the blue volume dial on my Fisher Price cassette tape player up to 10. Another scene: the keen, burning shame and frustration of struggling to pronounce certain sounds and words. Another clip: waking up from surgery in a children's ward, my mum by the bedside with a present. The strange scratch of the hospital gown.

I was six when a hole was made in my ear drum and grommets – tiny tubes – were inserted to encourage better air flow and prevent the build-up of liquid that had been hampering my hearing since I was a toddler. It was a fairly routine procedure for small children with what's commonly known as glue ear. The grommets are inserted and fall out of their own accord within a year, improving the patient's hearing and preventing recurrent ear infections.

Whatever deafness I experienced as a child fell away as I grew up, became a kind of footnote in the family history, sometimes a quip as to why I can grow loud when I am excited. It's neither hushed up nor talked about, simply a residue of childhood.

I'm newly curious about it, this time when I couldn't hear. It's become part of my life that was almost forgotten, yet I remember it looming large over my childhood. The lives we live – the decisions we make, the things that happen to us, the lovers we hold and the children we bear – are etched on our bodies. I wondered if what had happened to mine had changed how I listened.

I embark upon the drawn-out rabbit hole of accessing my medical history, and one afternoon 356 badly scanned pages land in my inbox in a zip file. My ears dominate: old-fashioned letters exchanged between consultant ENT surgeons and my GP, verdicts from speech therapists and audiologists. There are grainy copies of audiograms and tympanograms I can't make sense of. It's difficult to shake the sense of seemingly endless infections, trips to the doctor, visits with consultants, periods of review. According to these scans, once a bundle of papers, somewhere, I was a child who variously couldn't hear, heard distorted sound and hated loud noises. At the bottom of one audiogram, written by hand in a round cursive: 'she got quite upset when she thought we didn't believe her'. I was four. I'm surprised by the heft of it, this polite little fact. I think it's because it's still such a familiar feeling, that fear of not being believed or heard. So many of us feel like we are shouting into the air, waiting for connection.

Three decades later, I make an appointment and wait the two weeks for it to arrive. I see a doctor I've not met before; a man about my age, who probably spent his teenage years listening to the same bands that I did, and tell him I'm having problems with my hearing. I talk about the tinnitus. He looks in my ears with the same horn-shaped instrument that was used when I was small, and I bump into a bodily memory from that time as he gently tugs on my ear to make more space. He tells me he will refer me, but not to get too hopeful about anything being done. My age puts me in a hinterland: neither young nor old, I am trapped in a halfling body in an ailing system. It happens, he says, that people my age who had grommets suffer from the same kind of sounds that I do. It is as if they were introduced to help let more sound in, but now we swim among too much noise.

The Second Day of Spring, 5.22 a.m.

MY THIGHS, MY HIPS, are pushed back towards my shoulders. I am being folded in half. The baby's shoulders are stuck and my body must be contorted to give them up. I feel nothing; I am pushing but numb, relying on muscular instinct and intent. Then, a rush of hands and heads as a blue-white being is lifted over my face. Hello, little one – the words slip from my mouth. The doctor says she didn't manage to see what the sex was. I turn my head right, see my husband's face mere centimetres from mine, see the emotion raw and sodden painted across it. Enough tears for the both of us. The baby has been carried away and people have gathered around him – it's a boy, he's a boy – and after all that noise, the mechanical, shouting, overwhelming roar of the operating theatre, all I can hear is silence. The baby is not crying.

Seconds pass, perhaps minutes. However long it actually

is, it feels longer. Someone explains that the baby is a bit shocked from the delivery. I stare at the corner of the room, where people in blue are doing things to the newest person in London. He cries. The keening peal of a newborn rises like a bubble floating in a glass, up above the blood and shit I see being bundled into a ball of paper, above the doctors talking as they stitch me back together, above my husband, who stands up and goes to him. The baby cries and I feel it pressing into my skin. He cries and I register it in my hollowed-out gut before I can make sense of it in my brain. This is a noise that is quieter than a phone ringing but to me it is the loudest thing in the room; it will always be the loudest thing in a room. He cries for the first time, and I understand that this sound, this sound that I have never heard before, is one I know to my bones.

HOME SOUNDS

I'VE OFTEN SAID THAT I grew up in a loud house, but I think it was a home that was full rather than loud. Ours is a family that shouts, but in over-excitement rather than anger. We'd clamber over one another's conversations at the dinner table like we would reach across for salt or ketchup. The piano sat in the room at the other end of the hallway to the kitchen and while I sometimes had to be bribed to play it, I would sit and watch my brother release chords and riffs without instruction from either our parents or any music at all. My sister's clear, high vocals would drift up the stairs. Two enormous speaker stacks, dating from long before I was born, were to be played around carefully in the lounge. Sometimes a new music book would appear – the Beatles, James Taylor – and I would learn the words to 'Lady Madonna' or 'Sweet Baby James' by osmosis as those larger than me would play and sing to its notation. On Friday nights I'd hear the beats of *Later . . . with Jools Holland* drift through my bedroom floorboards. By Sunday morning, this was replaced by the bassline to *The Archers'* theme tune, the sonic accompaniment to the smell of potatoes roasting. My mother papered the downstairs loo in yellowed sheet music she'd bought for pennies at an auction and I became familiar with the crotchets and quavers of the bars that were at my eye-level.

We never defined as musical the way some families do, but music flowed constant and steady around us. Grade examinations and piano teachers, my mother's stories of playing 'Puff The Magic Dragon' to schoolchildren in the Seventies on her guitar. I was nudged into the church choir at eight, more out of community than religion, tugged the rough cotton of the smallest cassock over my head and learned to let descants out of my lungs and wrap archaic lyrics around my tongue. Around the same time, my brother brought the Spice Girls' debut album home from an exchange trip to America, where CDs were affordable. I remember the ritualistic thrill of being allowed to place it in the stereo, small fingers on the cheap plastic **PLAY** button, the sound of Mel B's footsteps and dirty giggle bouncing off the tiled floor in the kitchen.

The sound of home was more evident in its absence – when I went to friends' quieter houses, or on Sunday afternoons, when my siblings were out – than in its being. It changed with the years. Different broadcasters on the radio, different theme music on the television shows we watched and then stopped watching. Children grow up, make new kinds of noise. My childhood overheard one side of my adolescent sister's phone calls; my own adolescence was soundtracked by the particular tone of my phone receiving a text message. Decades on and the same jokes take up happy airspace, the laughter often pre-empting the punchline. So much of the sound of home is of the families — chosen and otherwise — that live there; to know those sounds as intimately as what breakfast cereal people like, or what their pet name is. When Matt and I found out we were going to have a child, I started to think about how I would change our home to accommodate them, to teach them and make them feel safe. I didn't necessarily think about what they might hear. But if we are taught how, and how not to, live by those who raised us, I learned that a certain kind of noise made a life: conversation around a table, the chatter of someone on the phone in the hallway and, often, music.

Twenty-five years after that Spice Girls CD and I am laying the sounds of the homes I have made over this one, as if they were made of tracing paper. Some things have been universal — always a table to eat at, always people around it. The burble of a boiling kettle; the dull, repetitive thud of knife on chopping board. The clatter of keys in a bowl. Conversation and the stillness of deep night, quiet enough for a light switch to puncture. Others have been less so. The years of sonic extremes of house-sharing, where there were many footsteps on the stairwell and clangs in the kitchen, but it was difficult to identify who they belonged to. Where sound systems would be set up for parties, but silence would reign during the day. Strange thuds of bedroom doors pulled-to in an attempt at privacy in a house of thin walls. The regular bumping of bike frames in a hallway.

I can pinpoint certain moments when the noises I live against stopped and started. Radio Four used to ripple through my pre-dawn mornings. For years I would stir to the sound of *Farming Today* and dress to the *Today* programme with such precision that I knew I was running late if I was around to hear 'Thought for the Day'. But I tuned it out during the anxious creep of Covid and it's yet to return. Radio has become a weekend thing instead, folded into the small rituals of papers on the table and eggs on the stove. Baby noise arrived in our home on the third day of spring and transformed all the air around it, softening voices and raising adrenaline and igniting delight. Certain shower songs and football chants and television theme tunes soundtracked momentous times in my life, but other sounds seemed to dissolve or vanish so gradually it took years to notice their absence.

One of the homes I made was quiet. There, an old lover and I made a life that was like an eggshell, clean and precise and fragile. I relished how immaculate it was, the big windows, the searing minimalism that comes with wearing an existence that is older than your years. Against its hard walls and tiled floors sound ricocheted and echoed, but I grew quieter and smaller within them. I have always sung; inexpertly, fully, because I like to open my mouth and follow a familiar melody, because I grew up around the people in my family singing, because it offers a release. But here I stopped. The man I lived with was riled by me singing. I think he found the unabashed freedom of it – the happy clumsiness of a repeated lyric or a missed note, this pure connection to something ingrained in me, the untrained shapes made by cords inside my throat – faintly embarrassing. And so I began to shrink my voice, singing only when he was out of the house. The singing stilled to a halt, and the music followed. At the same time, I started to splinter into different selves: the uneasy homemaker who tried to occupy a space that felt too grown-up for her; the girl who still wanted to stay out all night with her friends; the changeling that was trying to mask all the difficulties behind doors. Music had been something for me to cling to. Now I was being pulled away from it.

Over time, my music choices merged with his. The songs I loved were rarely played. I would sometimes listen through headphones, but it became easier just to stop entirely. The noises we made together filled in the space – laughter, yes, but also the cacophony of misunderstanding. I would shout in frustration, aggravated as much by his stubborn silence as he was by my singing, and wonder what the neighbours must think.

At the same time, music was becoming increasingly woven into my working hours. I had been made responsible for the newspaper's music reviews – researching and selecting which gigs to cover in which cities and making sure the right journalist was there to review them. The cost of 'missing' something was being found out publicly, when an editor looked through rival newspapers and wondered why we hadn't got the same high-profile review that they had. I swiftly learned that writing about music wasn't so much driven by passion as hierarchy and luck. Our judgement on whether an artist was good or not was trusted, but we had to back it up with our words and our knowledge. Sometimes I felt like I was sitting an endless quiz of pop cultural history; miss an album or a band and I would be discredited; somebody else would be sent to review a show instead.

There was never room for these vulnerabilities to show. The music industry remains wildly patriarchal: reports from the USC Annenberg Inclusion Initiative, founded by Dr Stacy L. Smith – arguably the leading academic researching inequality in the entertainment industry – have found that in the most popular songs of the past decade (according to the US Billboard Hot 100 Year End Chart) women make up barely more than 10 per cent of songwriters and a fifth of artists. On songs that charted between

2012 and 2021, less than 3 per cent of music producers were women. Women barely headline music festivals. In the UK, gains are being made, but at a glacial pace. Women suffer from the same glass ceiling as they age in the music industry as they do elsewhere, and start to leave this line of work in their mid-forties.

I used to report on these numbers. It was harder, though, to get people in the industry to speak about trying to exist in such a particularly patriarchal atmosphere; interviews with young artists were tightly controlled by their media teams – it was unusual that a fledgling pop star would want to make her name by citing sexist treatment. Music companies, awards and record labels made a big fuss of feminist artists, but many of those artists only found the courage to speak of what they'd been through – Rebecca Lucy Taylor of Self Esteem, for instance; Taylor Swift in her battle with Big Machine Records; Britney Spears and her conservatorship – after escaping the clutches of the industry that created and silenced them.

When stories caught alight – such as Phoebe Bridgers claiming, alongside other women, that she was a victim of an emotionally abusive relationship with Ryan Adams, who was 20 years her senior, considerably more established as a professional musician and called their time together 'a brief, consensual fling'; Kesha's eight-year-long legal battle with producer Dr Luke, which included accusations of emotional abuse and rape; RnB singer Casandra 'Cassie'

Ventura settling a suit with Sean Combes that alleged years of abuse and rape, among many, many others – they felt rare and deeply painful. They let out a crackle, a promise of change that is yet to become a reckoning. Young women are still at the mercy of a patriarchal industry upheld by history and power; the stories will keep coming, because so many female artists are put on stage and expected to be quiet about what they endured to get there.

I was lucky: I never experienced abuse – emotional or otherwise – from the music industry while working alongside it. Many other female music journalists have stories of being touched inappropriately while interviewing artists, suffering the drug-addled abuse of frustrated rock stars or being mistaken for a groupie among a sea of male technicians and roadies. But constantly inhabiting spaces that felt so keenly male was a slow, grinding thing. It is easy to feel small as a short woman in a crowd of men. I became accustomed to being one of a handful of young women in the press tent at festivals, getting barked at for having the temerity to sit at a desk an older, male photographer had marked out as his with a Sharpie. I learned the coarse, arrogant language of our male music critics in order to reason with them, to persuade them into doing their job, to deliver their edits. I grew a kind of invisible armour. As my workplace gradually made women in senior roles redundant, I kept company with men and wondered where my role models were. Silently, I lobbied for access to the boys' club. I still don't know if I ever gained entry.

In hindsight, I was part of the problem: one of the many young, female journalists sent out to ask young, female artists about their experience in the industry, but never asking male artists what they were doing to gain equity. I would push to promote more female artists in our pages and be repeatedly turned down, or questioned about what their photos looked like, whether we could take our own. Eventually the effort seemed too much; I stopped trying. I stopped listening to music, too. It was easier to subscribe to the norm, review and write about the same artists we always had.

Just as certain sounds drifted into my life, music drifted out of it. For all that my life was full of noise, I had made it quiet of music. When Matt got up early with the baby he would put the radio on; at that time in the morning there were upbeat dance songs. When I would enter the kitchen – after quietly getting up or working at my desk – it would feel like a bombardment of noise. These were songs I was familiar with, songs I had danced to, songs I knew the words of, but they felt like an assault. The loudness in my life lived in pockets; when I was by myself, when I was alone, I preferred quiet.

If I tried to unpick how I had grown from a girl who thrived among the dissonance of a punk record into a woman who preferred to be in silence, I got caught in tangles. The narratives of my life layered up like the skeins of sound from an orchestra tuning up. I tried to straighten them out: the man who made me feel small for singing; the job that challenged my enthusiasm for new music; every single speaker and gig and headphone that left a ghost of itself in my ear canal.

This could have had nothing to do with any of it. This might have been what my body was destined to do: retreat from the sounds it once stretched out to. Without the people I love in it, my life would be a quiet one: kettle boiling, knives chopping, keyboard tapping, tinnitus ringing, a siren passing by. Add in the overture of those people – the WhatsApp voice notes, the warm greetings at the door, the squeaking of the baby in the mornings, his splashing in the bath at night, the snatches of song sung by my husband, my mum on speakerphone – and it strengthened. Where was I, who was I, in all of this? I didn't know what I was adding to the chorus.

The Third Day of Spring

WE BRING HIM HOME ON a windy, overcast day. There are no cabs around, so we take him on the bus, brand new. Open the door and show him around; dump the bags; pick up the post. The first night – the one I remember in snatches – he won't be put down without crying, so we take it in shifts. But once he allows it, we tuck him under blankets in a soft basket next to the bed. I lie between him and my husband, stirring to search for the baby's breath. Too fearful of waking him to switch on the light, I gingerly crane my neck over the basket – my body is still a mess of blood and thread – and turn an ear to his little open mouth.

Newborns don't always breathe regularly and in the seconds of silence between the tiny, gentle pants I feel my heart rate stiffen. For a moment the whole dark world is here, in a couple of centimetres between us, waiting for the sound of air passing. Sylvia Plath called it 'moth-breath' and the fluttering is the same, the sound stilling as an insect may close its wings before taking flight. Her poem 'Morning Song' translates the first new days of motherhood into those of noises, of wet skin on skin and cries and echoes and notes.

As the days pass his moth-breath evolves. There are exhalations and snores, a few weeks when a sound like a screech owl's cry emerges from the basket. In time, he grows too large for the basket and we move him into a cot in another room. I relish the quiet – no more will I wake for the small, high sounds he makes in his sleep, when nothing is the matter but his dreams. I watch his body rise and fall through the baby monitor instead. Funny: my husband never woke when the baby cried next to our bed, but does when the noise is filtered through the electronic microphone and speaker of this domestic surveillance. We soon learn to switch the sound off and leave the bedroom door open, knowing that I will wake when he cries. I used to sleep through everything – people shouting outside the window, sirens, thunderstorms – but my body moves itself out of bed within seconds now, my brain catching up after.

I am exhausted, I could sleep for days, I dream of lying in a floatation tank for more than five hours at a time. But I am programmed into this noise and I am programmed into its absence, too. When the baby sleeps for eight, nine, even 10 hours, my body wakes up anyway. This silence is perhaps the most intense, both jubilant and lonely. I struggle to return to sleep, expecting him to wake as soon as I do. Instead, I lie in this emptiness, listening to everything and nothing all at once, waiting for the noise to rear up again.

INNER VOICE

My understanding of quietude was growing more intimate and complicated as I spent more time in it. Silence, I was beginning to realise, could be as noisy as it could be quiet. I was fortunate to be less familiar with a more punishing kind of silence, the one born of isolation and fear, although I had felt it when my child was wrenched out of me without making a sound and in the house, in the dead of night, when he was asleep and I was not despite being wracked with tiredness. This was a silence in which the worst thoughts would grow. But the silence I knew better was a broader, more malleable thing. Sometimes my life felt silent because of an absence of things – of invitations and nights out, of the music that had soundtracked the woman I was, of communication from friends who now felt at a remove even though I didn't feel I had changed that much. This wasn't true silence; I simply lived a life that housed another kind of noise. Still, it often felt as if I spent a lot of time with the relentless racket of my own thoughts. My body and brain had undergone a change that nobody could explain to me before it happened; it often felt like I was piecing things back together.

I was learning that there were types of silence that can change your life, that can rewire how your brain navigates sound. Claire had been in labour for three days when the doctors decided to turn the baby around inside her so she could push him out. 'We were at the point where he needed to just be delivered now, because he couldn't take any more,' she tells me. We're sitting on the square blocks of her sofa, beneath a window that lets in a meagre midday light, cups of tea between our palms. It's nearly Christmas; there's a nativity scene on her windowsill. Tiny socks hang on an airer in the corner of the living room. Claire gave birth to her first child, the one that changed how her world sounded, three and a half years ago now. It was traumatic, and it's only later that I learn this is the first time she's spoken about it.

Claire's son was born unresponsive. In the absence of his cry, her relationship to sound – the very way in which she listened – transformed completely. 'When he was out they lifted him up and he was totally limp and an unseemly colour,' she says. 'Like, not just your average blue, he was basically grey. And he made no sound whatsoever. I was waiting to hear the sound, of course, you wait to hear the sound. And there was nothing except, "Fast bleep the reg" – as in the registrar. Then I heard this "thwack" sound, which was like a rope on water, and it was the sound of my blood hitting the floor. From then on, I couldn't see anything, or taste anything or feel anything. But I could hear everything that was happening.' Claire recalls it like it was a script – her words; she tells me that's how it exists in her memory. The panicked conversations of the medics about her blood loss and how to control it, the sound of them resuscitating her son, the horrified silence of her husband standing behind her. 'It was three minutes and forty-seven seconds until he made a sound,' she says. 'And to be honest, part of me genuinely thought that he died in the few minutes where this procedure had been happening and the monitoring was off. And I had a small thought to myself that I should have left notes, I should have left notes of what to do for his funeral. Because, I thought, he'll be gone, and I'll just take my own life as soon as I come around from this.'

Later, in the high dependency unit, Claire noticed that everything had become very loud. She could hear her baby, says she remembers the sound of his tiny hand landing on her chest, but she was also newly aware of a surreally large spectrum of sound in the hospital ward. 'I could hear all of these monitors, and all of the footsteps and the noise of the curtains being pulled back and forth, of the horrible rustling of the mat you sit on after birth.

And I was like, "I'm sure this will calm down. It's just an initial response to nearly dying." But it never went away, and still I experienced life, my sound life, with that same intensity – as if I've just almost died, as if he's almost died and been brought back to life.' People often say that the day their child is born is among the happiest of their lives, Claire continues. 'But there was no happiest day in my life. No way. It was just the day everything got incredibly loud.'

The baby survived – he's now a happy, healthy pre-schooler with a large vocabulary and a predilection for insects. Claire describes her condition as 'postpartum misophonia', a particularly extreme sensitivity to sound that has radically altered how she lives. 'Day-to-day noises, which are part of life, are amplified so much that they become intolerable,' she explains. I ask her to give me some examples. 'Typing is a massive one; typing is thunderous to me,' she says. 'Mouse-clicking. People turning light switches on and off. Mouth-breathing. Snoring. See, I sound very unreasonable!' she laughs. 'But I would find it impossible to work in an office on a regular basis at this point.'

I have known – and not-known – Claire for nearly 25 years by the time we sit here, on her sofa, a few days before Christmas. We were best friends in secondary school who had drifted out of one another's lives by our early twenties. Twelve years later she got back in touch, and our friendship fizzed and sparked back into life. It's been a telescoping thing to rekindle, to learn about huge parts of a life belonging to someone whose adolescence you were so familiar with. Our friendship weathered and sustained our teenage years; we navigated what it was to grow out of childhood and into something else. It feels fitting that it should pick up again at a time when we are changing once more: both matrescent, both working out how our bodies work, both trying to survive something that is entirely mundane and completely extraordinary. When she sent me a WhatsApp voice note for the first time, I recognised her voice as intimately as if I had heard a forgotten song on the radio and realised I still knew all of the words. She always was, she tells me, a person who was 'alive to sound'. Claire has always loved accents and enjoyed voices; as a child she would enjoy the action of rubbing two pieces of paper together just to hear the rustle they would make; it relaxed her. I challenge her to divvy up her sensory experience of the world into percentages and she instantly tells me that, before having her two children, sound comprised 60 per cent of her lived experience – every other sense was given an equal 10 per cent.

'I used to have quite a noisy life,' she says. She'd find the radio soothing, and learn a lot of things by listening to it; would have it on even as she played music and watched television. None of these noises would prevent her from also being able to, say, write an email or read a book. 'I mean, this sounds completely insane,' Claire admits. 'But yeah, it would just be fine to have, like, a radio play and also music, and also have a conversation with somebody; that wouldn't be an issue to me. I could segment that off and be all right with that.'

It was on the radio, about three months after her son was born, that Claire first learned that misophonia was something that could affect neurotypical people – sound sensitivity is frequently associated with neurodivergence. 'The researcher of the study they were covering said, "When you start to hear the sound, the problematic sound, you need to gnash your teeth together. Simply gnash teeth together, and you will find relief from the sound." I did try it. I still do. It doesn't quite have the effect, though. But it's a similar principle [to what I do], I think: that this is a motion that can distract you.' Claire has developed her own strategies: she drinks her tea very hot, for instance, so she can access the heat of a mug if need be – just as she is doing as she speaks to me, to concentrate on our conversation rather than the sound of the white noise machines playing to keep our children asleep upstairs. 'There's a kind of internal soundproofing where you try to feel things less, almost like you try to compensate by concentrating on how another sense feels.' Without this soundproofing, the noises Claire hears manifest as a physical pressure. 'I start to feel like I'm going to get a migraine, but instead of the visual auras people experience during migraine, I experience more of a sound aura. It's very noisy, but the sounds are all internal and intrusive. I've not let myself think about the origin of the sounds properly, because it's too much to bear. But it's probably the sounds from the time [of her son's birth]. Let's call them intrusive sounds.' It's when she starts hearing the beginnings of these intrusive sounds that she interrupts them with a physical motion, such as teeth gnashing. I ask how often this happens. 'Oh, probably ten, twelve times a day.'

She thought giving birth to her daughter – who arrived bawling – might be 'sonically redemptive, but it wasn't. It just continued, my capacity for sound expanded.' The children are close together in age, and Claire thinks, in hindsight, her continued sensitivity to sound was tied to her matrescence: 'I needed to listen for both of them because they were so small. They both needed me quite heavily, so I had to listen out for the two different pitches.' In time, she says, her body took over; what she had to do consciously was 'maintain control, not being completely overwhelmed by the sounds of everything'.

Claire exists in a funny paradox of silence and jarring noise now. There's no television in her house; the radio was turned off years ago. 'Anybody else who lived my life would find it so quiet. We even moved [from a city] to a small village, because I wanted a more peaceful life.' It is painful, she admits, to talk about how much she removes from her life because of the sensory overload. 'I know that my children's lives are impacted by my inability to cope with the noise of life. I don't take them to museums as much as I would, because the echoing just really does something to me, I find that difficult. Toddler groups are a total nightmare, but I do it because I actually really like small children and babies.' I bring up the paper rustling: would this be something soothing for her now? 'I think, honestly, to find a sound pleasurable would be very difficult for me. I can't even contemplate it, to be honest.'

As we talk, Claire reminds me of things I had forgotten. Of how present music was in our friendship, of the hours that we would spend lying on her bed, listening to music or singing along to MTV. I remember the stupid voices and accents we'd talk to one another in, how we would make sounds with our bodies and turn them into play, transform them into in-jokes that would render us useless with laughter, shrink the whole thing down into a tiny, hilarious reference. She reminds me that I never could listen to music and read a book at the same time, like she could. That listening, for me, was often an active pursuit. 'We used to listen to music intimately,' she says. 'That was very normal: talking, and singing, and listening – they were all just interchangeable. It was very, very easy to listen with you.'

Those memories, of that feverish appetite we had for music as teenagers, of our abilities to give our full selves, our full bodies, to it, are fond for both of us, for all they seem obscure. Neither of us listen much to the music we used to; we've got out of the habit of seeking it out for our own pleasure. I mention that I'd looked up a particular choral piece I'd been craving on YouTube a few days earlier, the novelty of feeling my entire body prickle up in goosebumps, how I'd sat at the kitchen table and pulled back the video slider to hear it tumble out of my inadequate laptop speakers again and again. 'I don't think I can let myself feel that,' Claire says. 'Because these are the kind of sound responses I used to have, you know, when we were teenagers. I can't feel that now. I can't let myself feel that I'm not . . . you know . . .' she trails off. 'Maybe I don't want to damage the memory of it.'

I think I understand, I tell her. I mention the strange queasiness I feel when bands I loved as a teenager pop up on festival bills curated to appeal to people my age, that I wouldn't want to chase the ghost of something. 'I would only be able to occupy the person I was then,' I tell her. Perhaps, I say, it would expose the absence of it in my life now. 'Maybe that's something I regret or I grieve or I mourn in some capacity that I haven't been able to acknowledge,' I say. 'Like, how did I let that die?' Is it something that's dead, Claire replies. I suppose, I reply, I'm trying to find that out.

•

I don't think I have made time to mourn what music used to be in my life. That might be what I am doing now — not trying to recapture it so much as acknowledge that it has become something different, and trying to accept that. When I was younger, music allowed me to inhabit a societal place that felt good. Since becoming pregnant I've felt portioned off into places I don't recognise or always want to be. My life plays out in different hours now: I spend the pre-dawn hours either sleeping or awake, caring for a baby. I used to find freedom and acceptance on club dance floors and among crowds of people; I relished that communion of bodies and voices crying out as they let something go. Now I spend a lot of time in a small, fiercely tight-knit unit: mother, baby, husband, friends, family. I am still navigating moments of release; they come in hours of sleep that are longer than I am expecting, or in the bliss of connection with my growing boy. But my body has been twisted into new shapes: shoulders hunched by carrying and feeding, hips shunted, knees rotated in by holding. I have not moved for reasons beyond necessity for so long. I have not raised my hands in the air in ecstasy. I feel cut off from those who do, I feel invisible to them. I know what their world looks like — I used to enter it — but they have no knowledge of the deep hush of mine. I seek to listen — and to connect through listening — as a means of joining these things up. Of finding a way to align my body with the dopamine rush of music and the corporeal thrill of dance; of putting the unspeakable intimacy and searing bliss of child-raising on a stage I can bear witness to. I want to make the quiet loud.

MISOPHONIA

I ARRIVE AT THE COLLEGE early and sit on a bench by the door. Linacre is one of Oxford's newest colleges; tucked away from the substantial limestone and iron gates of the university's better-known buildings, it occupies a sprawling red-brick structure that calls to mind a country club or old-fashioned holiday resort. I'm here to meet Jane Gregory, a clinical psychologist who has a Wellcome fellowship here. Established in the early Sixties, Linacre was founded as an experiment, with a vision of a 'new type of society': it was the first graduate college in the country that welcomed men and women, regardless of what they studied. And Jane is similarly pushing boundaries: she's trying to find a pioneering way of treating misophonia – a condition in which people have disproportionately strong reactions to certain sounds.

Claire couldn't, I reasoned, have been alone in her world of noise. After all, she'd heard of misophonia on the radio;

there were other people living as she did, in an external world kept purposefully quiet, and an internal one that could be deafening. But the condition is still on the cusp of medical awareness: the term wasn't even formally coined until 2001. Since then, scientific papers on misophonia have gradually snowballed from three articles in 2006 to 36 in 2021, with the bulk of misophonia research published in the past two years. Jane, who experiences misophonia, is among the handful of researchers and psychologists who are trying to create a new way of diagnosing, understanding and treating misophonia. I've come to visit her – at this slightly scruffy, lightly institutional building in Oxford – to find out more about the disorder.

Like Claire, like most people with misophonia, Jane didn't realise that her experience of sound was unusual until she found out more about it for herself. She's in her mid-forties, open and wry; her auburn curls hold a little dampness and she's almost as unfamiliar with Linacre's inner workings as I am – she mostly works from home nearby, where she's set up a quiet space away from the television and speakers used by her young family on a daily basis. We sit in the corner of one of the college's common rooms, next to the fading afternoon light from a pair of French windows. Jane has become something of a poster girl for misophonia: she's the author of *Sounds Like Misophonia*, a book that offers practical therapeutic methods of dealing with the condition, and a website of the same name that lists the broadsheet newspapers and national broadcast appearances she's made talking about intolerable everyday noises. Misophonia may have been an unknowable, if looming, presence in her life since childhood (she quips that she once threw her brother's doughnut in the bin because she so hated the sound of him eating), but it's come to define her adulthood.

'My brain works wonderfully when it's quiet,' she tells me. 'I can be really productive and I can figure things out and problem solve.' But when there's a noise – a clock ticking, for instance, or a dripping tap or the clicking of someone's pen – it completely derails Jane's ability to focus. 'The gap between how my brain functions when it's quiet and how it functions when there's a clock in the room is so vast that it becomes a source of anger for me; I feel like I'm a different person,' she explains. Jane was in her thirties and working as a clinical psychologist in the NHS, with a specialism in OCD, when she encountered the term 'misophonia'. Her hypersensitivity to sound, she believes, has aided her as a therapist: 'If someone has a subtle change in their tone, that could be a sign that their emotion has changed. Even if they're not showing emotion, I can detect that change, and I won't ignore it, and I'll raise it when it feels like something has changed.'

After stumbling into Facebook groups of people who shared her experience, she 'saw how much people were suffering, and especially people who weren't in the privileged position that I was in, where I could make choices about where I lived and who I spent time with: I was a manager so I could go into an office if I needed to, for instance. They were really suffering because they just weren't in control of this at all.' When she looked into research around misophonia, she was struck by the sheer absence of it, and how she could potentially change that, given her experience in research. Quite swiftly, Jane began to make connections between her clinical practice and the need for greater research and treatment provision around misophonia. She contacted other researchers, experimented with CBT techniques on her own experience of misophonia and pulled together a proposal for her boss. 'By coincidence, someone had been referred to the clinic who had misophonia,' she said, and so she proposed working on some treatment ideas based on her findings. It went well – well enough that her clinic began to accept referrals for similar cases.

This was important in itself: there had previously been little to no clinical treatment of misophonia in the UK. But Jane also began work on creating a formal measurement for the condition, something that would help to capture its complexities, establish how it became a disorder and better equip practitioners to treat people who lived with it. Psychometrician Dr Silia Vitoratou was in labour with her daughter when she emailed Jane. Silia – who also has misophonia – had been developing the questionnaire that would become the Selective Sound Sensitivity Syndrome Scale (S-Five).

'She looked me up,' Jane says. 'At the time I'd written a few blog posts about doing experiments on my own misophonia as a CBT therapist. She was reading my blog, she found it funny – she said it helped her get through this really long, extended period of labour. So the birth of our collaboration was literally the same day as the birth of her daughter.' They met when Silia's daughter was a few weeks old: Silia 'brought this tiny little baby, and we chatted and both have really similar ideas. I was coming at it from a clinical perspective, looking at stuff that had been developed already, and she was from a statistics and psychometrics perspective: the idea of measuring things that can't be directly observed.'

Together, Jane and Silia worked together to try and document, for the first time, the lived experience they both knew so deeply. Along with two female research assistants, they gathered 100 statements about misophonia from their research, from the scant scientific papers and the hours spent delving into misophonia forums, from the patients they'd seen with misophonia and their own experiences. They surveyed thousands of participants with misophonia, and from there they produced a list of 25 statements that capture how misophonia manifests. The statements form a questionnaire – the S-Five – which relates to the five different factors of misophonia. They are: externalising ('I get angry at other people because of how disrespectful they are with the noises they make'); internalising ('The way I react to certain noises makes me feel like I must be an unlikeable person deep down'); impact ('I can see a future where I cannot do everyday things because of my reactions to noises'); outburst ('Some sounds are so unbearable that I will shout at people to make them stop'); and threat ('I feel trapped if I cannot get away from certain noises'). The S-Five has since been translated and rolled out across the world and tested on different populations: in the Mandarin-speaking Chinese population, in German, in Portuguese-speaking populations. Work is currently under way on a Farsi sample. 'Now we can see that there's cultural differences in the terms of nature of the reaction and the types of sounds,' Jane explains, 'but what keeps emerging is a cross-cultural consistency in terms of the five aspects we've captured.' In essence: while the sounds and people's outward responses to them may differ across cultures, the ways that misophonia manifests (uncontrollable emotions due to sound; feelings of guilt or resentment due to sound; life being limited due to reactions to sound; having or fearing aggressive outbursts due to sound) remain the same. 'Silia's never seen something that's so consistent across cultures,' Jane says. 'It's pretty amazing.'

The women did a lot of this initial work in their own

time. 'I really enjoyed it, but it was annoying not being paid,' Jane laughs. When she started applying for grants to receive funding she was repeatedly turned down. 'No one had heard of it,' she says. 'None of the funding bodies cared. They were like, "Why would we fund this? We don't even know what it is."'

Jane won a fellowship after a tip-off about her current research supervisor, someone she was told likes 'supporting clinicians to become researchers' and 'wacky things'. She applied, and was awarded funding to complete a three-year research project on misophonia. As Jane writes on her website: 'I'm not expecting to find a cure. I'm hoping my research will help to develop strategies to reduce the intensity of misophonia reactions and to help those who struggle with misophonia to live a more fulfilling life.'

Already, Jane's work – carried out alongside her job as an NHS clinician and her caring duties to her two young children – has been making an impact. In raising the profile of misophonia from something nobody had heard of, she has enabled other people who live with it – like Claire – to realise that they are not alone or broken. 'Most people who find me do so because they've found the word that describes the condition they have experienced their whole life,' she tells me. 'I have a handwritten letter from a woman in her nineties in New Zealand. It was simply addressed to "Jane Gregory, Clinical Psychology, Oxford", and it found its way through the university. She had read about the research that we published last year, which got a bit of press coverage, and was writing to thank me for my work. She said she had felt like a freak her whole life, felt guilty about decisions she made as a parent, and was reassured to read about my research and discover the term misophonia. Moments like that,' Jane said, 'it sort of validates everything I'm working on.'

Jane's research with Silia has found misophonia to be surprisingly common: from data collected in a representative sample from the UK, 18 per cent had what their team would consider misophonia – 'which is not just that they get annoyed by sounds, but they get that intense feeling of being trapped and helpless when they are stuck with the sounds, that they need to escape, or they get the urge to escape, and have to change the way that they live their life because of it'. It seems a huge portion of society to me, to be living invisibly in an unbearably loud world. Jane puts another spin on it: 'That idea of it being nearly one in five people, I think that that makes sense. It's like, for a social species to survive, some people would be more tuned into sounds, and some people were more tuned into visuals. And some people are really good at tuning those things out, and they're the people who will be focusing on looking after the children and won't be getting distracted by the sounds.' There are times in our lives when our brain grows more sensitive to sound automatically, she points out: 'If you're walking home late at night, even if you're walking in busy traffic, you can hear if there are footsteps behind you. You don't tune it out if you think that it might be a threat.

'And I think,' she continues, 'people with misophonia have that in times where there is no threat, and their brain is telling them that there is. And so it feels unsettling. It makes them feel angry because it feels like a violation, even though this person isn't really doing anything wrong. Some people go through experiences like that. Parenthood is a really good example of that: you're supposed to listen out for changes in your baby's breathing, and so you will ignore other things and tune into your baby. When new parents try to have a conversation, they can tell if it's their child making a fuss over there and will automatically turn and deal with it. There are periods where that's a really healthy thing to do and helps us survive, but some people get stuck there and some people have always been stuck there. And for some reason, the brain doesn't tell you; when you realise that it's safe, your brain doesn't update.'

I think about Claire and the near-four minutes she spent listening out for her son's cry as she haemorrhaged on an operating table, all of her other senses fading as she grasped for a sign of his survival. I think about her moving to the countryside, her regret over not taking her children to more museums because they are too loud. I think of how isolating it must be to feel such claustrophobia from noise; of the women struggling to sleep next to their snoring partners, or finding ways to navigate the cacophony of daily life all the while feeling like something is wrong with them. I think of Jane's theory, that from an evolutionary standpoint, there would be more people to share the mental and physical load of keeping our communities safe, of listening out for danger and of looking after our children. Only, now we don't raise our young in packs, but often alone, against an ever-increasing tidal wave of domestic sound.

For a long time, Jane tells me, it was assumed that women were more predisposed to misophonia – there were always a lot more women in misophonia studies, who were willing to stand up and speak about the fact that life sounded louder to them. But her research has found no difference in its prevalence or severity between men and women. Differences were found, she said, in the five factors: men were a little bit more likely to have an outburst, or fear having an outburst, and women were slightly more likely to internalise and feel like it was their fault, but these differences were very small and there was no overall difference in prevalence. And yet it was an all-female team, nearly all of whom had misophonia, who gave up their time to develop a means of capturing this lived experience, and women were more likely to volunteer – often for free – to participate in studies; most show that, unless there was a deliberate attempt to make the sample representative of the gender distribution of the population, there were usually more women than men taking part. All to continue to research and quantify something that defined their lives, but which few established funding bodies thought legitimate enough to warrant financing.

Jane tells me that she's thinking a lot about context in her work: why the sound of a small child rustling a crisp packet on a train wouldn't trigger as strong a reaction as if an adult was making that noise. She tells me about the year she spent as a teenage exchange student, swapping the school she attended in her 'fairly small town' in Australia for a private prep school in Los Angeles. Jane was the kind of girl whose academic prowess was built into her identity – it's partly why she found the impact of noise on her ability to study so problematic – but at home she studied alongside other teenagers who didn't care much about their grades. In America, though, 'everyone was planning to go to university, everyone cared about their marks and everyone celebrated each other's successes. I had this year where that part of what defined me was now being celebrated rather than criticised, and I noticed that I was hardly bothered by sounds in the classroom that year.' This realisation only occurred to her 'much, much later', when she was thinking about misophonia more conceptually.

In these realms – where background noises are distractingly loud, and the volume of everyday things renders a supposed silence an isolating din – the acts of listening and being seen overlap. Living with misophonia is to exist alongside a funhouse-mirror experience of sound, where the noises that are often tuned out by the non-misophonic are so large as to be life-changing. In some ways it is a microcosm of navigating life in a female body, endlessly subject to a trap of opinions on how we should exist, just trying to find a means of doing it that feels vaguely comfortable.

Recognition, though, can make these experiences less lonely. In hearing misophonia discussed on the radio, Claire was able to name her experience; in reading about Jane's work, a grandmother on the other side of the world was able to contextualise a motherhood that had taken place six decades earlier. I felt seen when the midwife turned up the heart rate monitor when I was in theatre; I felt seen, and I felt listened to without having spoken a word. If listening could lead to connection, then silence can exist even among the realms of noise for those whose experience isn't acknowledged or recognised. Jane's work is still in its infancy, still fighting for long-term funding and mainstream recognition, but already she is making life less noisy for those who find even silence too loud. Silence can be peaceful for the privileged, but it can be lonely for those who are longing. Claire and Jane and Silia had found means of naming their unspoken experience of listening, but this suggested that silence – and noise – could show up in all sorts of ways that societal establishments hadn't felt worthy of acknowledging. If listening better meant connecting with the unrepresented, the unwritten and the unseen, then we needed to do better at naming what is heard. We needed to establish that we experience things that are invisible and uncommon, that this transforms how we live, and that those lives aren't often accommodated – but we might all benefit from understanding better how they exist. I didn't have misophonia, but I often felt as if I was transforming in ways that society suggested I should keep secret: that I must remedy the marks my baby left on my body, smooth over the snags of my 'baby brain', turn the raw and grisly reality of my matresence into a lighthearted joke, lest the reality of it be too confronting. I had been fortunate: in reaching out two weeks after I had my son, Claire had offered me a kind of dialect for communicating my experience. If we had made a tangled web of a love language as teenagers, we set about forming another now we had grown. In the smallest hours and on the most frustrating days, she offered me a way of naming the noise.

The Last Day in May

THE HIGH STREET IS ALIGHT with glitter. Tonight, it is a catwalk. Beyoncé Knowles-Carter has arrived in London and the neighbourhood has given itself over to her. Her music blasts out of cars; her face appears grainy on the homemade T-shirts of staff in McDonald's. The pageantry has begun. A queen is coming.

Beyoncé will perform in the football stadium that looms over the squat, down-at-heel high street. I have been here before on match day, dwarfed by the crowds of men in anoraks their wives bought them, silenced by the low, spittled chants that ripple among the terraces. Now it is nearly summer, the footballers are elsewhere and the happenings at the stadium have choked up the trains in this part of town. Fans – female fans – fill up the Underground platforms with perfume and chatter, and form tight, frustrated crowds outside train stations; everyone is running late, everyone is trying to make it.

THE LAST DAY IN MAY

The sullen men in big coats have been replaced with glistening bodies.

I wait outside the entrance for my friend and watch people take photos in front of the screens that adorn the stadium, holding an image of the singer in a scanty silver bikini on a horse, rotating like a ballerina in a jewellery box. I see silver lamé pulled across chests and thighs, sequins draped from hip to tarmac, snakeskin and bumbags and Stetsons with tassels bought from a haberdasher's and glued on in devotion. A beautiful boy walks past me, biceps in bouclé, freckles from cheekbone to cheekbone. A man – a local, not going to the concert – walks against the endless flow of the well-dressed, holding his phone aloft. His astonishment is loud enough to hear in spite of it all: 'Oh my God.'

It is dislocating. In the past eight weeks, I have only left the house after seven p.m. once. I gave birth two months earlier; my body is strange and puffy with the ghosts of pregnancy. I don't realise it yet, but my brain is still fogged up, like a window. I feel deeply, keenly alive in a way I've not for months. I feel alone in a way I never thought possible. Outside the stadium, watching hundreds of people celebrate a moment they have been waiting for – Beyoncé has not played in London for five years – I feel otherworldly. I do not know what to wear or how to be. In two little life-altering months I have softened into something made of milk and blood and salt. It feels so hard here. It feels like a different plane of existence, rather than a pavement at the other end of a Tube line.

We funnel through the flat grey corridors of the stadium and emerge into its maw, opposite the stage. We have tickets to a part of the stadium that sets it apart from its rivals. It's called the Wall of Sound, an uninterrupted run of seating built to contain and amplify the shouting of those occupying it. Players have said that at times the noise coming from this part of the stadium is so loud it is difficult to hear their teammates. Tonight, we will be standing here and we will be making the noise.

There are minutes to spare, and the anticipation of thousands of people sounds like an orchestra keying up to play. It's still light when the speakers kick in, dropping the lush polyphony that ushers Beyoncé's appearance on stage. It's loud enough to drown out the screaming. She appears, refined in a ball-gown, and when she opens her mouth with a soft admission of love it sounds so perfect it verges on hyper-reality.

The show lasts nearly three hours. Every 30 minutes a new theme, a new outfit, a new tone to manoeuvre us into increasingly dizzying new stratospheres. The pace of it all is wild and relentless. I had forgotten what it is like, to inhabit a fantasy dreamt up by a brain as purely creative and as lavishly funded as this.

To take it all in from these seats feels like standing on the edge of a precipice, as if the rest of the stadium is the sea and we are on a cliff-face, being battered by the wind. At times, it reminds me of being on a rollercoaster; there is something guttural and gravity-defying about the sudden peaks and troughs of the music: a searing, reaching harmonic high, a plummet of bass. Sometimes it is a physical thing; that combination of feeling the air temperature cool beneath a darkening May sky and the reverb of speakers vibrating hundreds of metres away. A muscular reflex kicks in with the dance beats and I find a grin plastered across my face with the sheer euphoria of it; I feel like an outsider, I can't entirely believe I am here and not at home next to my sleeping baby, and yet I am also the same person, the same body, who once let herself go to the pounding of dance music.

Occasionally a hush descends and it is always unexpected and odd. In a couple of weeks, as the tour continues, audiences will actively challenge themselves to silence a stadium at a specific part of a song at Beyoncé's command, but for now it only happens as a kind of respite. We are briefly cocooned by it; in the breathers between costume changes and sections, the intimacy of people's nights out presents itself: I hear snatches of conversations, can isolate the choral layers of the backing track.

But then there are moments, especially when Beyoncé sings a cappella, swapping the accompaniment of her band for that of her audience, when this vertiginous slide of plastic seats becomes a kind of instrument in itself, a vessel of air and vibration making notes in unison. When this happens, the effect carries a ghost of that heavy animism of the chants that I first heard in this cavernous space.

The world's most famous pop star is playing at this venue because it is modern and capacious, but it's nevertheless subversive. *Renaissance* is an album – and a tour – dedicated to celebrating Blackness and queerness, to the cultures that marginalised people have fashioned around themselves in defiance and identity. The Wall of Sound was not created to carry the noise made by thousands of women and gay men; it was not built to reflect the word **FEMINISM** at the other end of the stadium. This place was made to hold footballers – male footballers – and their fans. And yet here I am, watching an homage to the Harlem ball scene play out: dancer Darius Hickman voguing in a baby-pink peplumed catsuit, chaps and heeled thigh-high boots. It feels rebellious and glorious and like the right kind of noise. Among the fug of matrescence I start to feel something awaken, almost as if the synapses in my brain that had grown dull with fatigue and hormones are beginning to spark back into communion.

In time, I feel the tug of a distant evacuation cord from the other side of the city; I have to leave, I don't want to be among the mass of glittering bodies leaving the stadium. I have to return to my child, lie next to him and listen out for his breathing in the quiet of our bedroom. But something has connected during the concert, whether it was the melodic rise of the instruments or the glissando of Beyoncé's vocals or, it feels more likely, the reverberations of being among tens of thousands of other bodies using themselves as instruments for excitement and release. This is about more than music; I am not moved to put *Renaissance* on after the show, just as I'd not been motivated to play it before I went. Instead, I have felt myself key into a more bodily expression of sound. The hyperreal perfection of Beyoncé's unaccompanied opening number sits in the same realm, I realise, as the rumbling hiss of the football chants I'd heard in the same place many months before. Sound as something created – and interpreted – by our bodies. Sound that is powerful enough to unlock something in mine.

GHOSTS

When the baby was three weeks old, I took him to a cinema screening that welcomed mothers with infants and learned that everyone else's child cried more quietly than mine. As the weeks passed, other mothers with newer babies arrived and fussed over their children when they were needy and I realised that my child's cry just sounded louder to me. A decibel reading would have suggested that the vast majority of the babies all cried at a similar volume. Your own will always feel louder.

In theory, at least, we emerge from the womb crying – and it takes months for those peals and mewls of survival to mellow into other, less alarming noises. Still, despite crying being an almost universal aspect of existence, it wasn't studied academically for centuries. In the 1980s Dr Kathleen Wermke, a global authority on the early vocal and language development in infants, started recording the sounds babies made. At that point, many researchers believed crying to be no more complex than a biological alarm signal, something to examine only if there were problems, such as the extensive and unexplained crying of colic. It was mothers who supported Wermke's research when the scientific community couldn't get behind it; they understood Wermke's belief that all parents had an instinctive ability to identify and react to their babies' cries. Research has since looked at what happens to parents' brains when their infants cry, finding that the parts of our brains associated with the need to move and speak are activated within 100 milliseconds of hearing the cry. There were greater neural responses in mothers than in those people who didn't have children; our brains are reprogrammed to respond before we've even had a chance to think about it. This might sound primeval – and it is wired into our biology – but even the noisy overwhelm of modern life can't drown out a baby's cry. It is a sound that is fundamentally designed to sear through everything else.

I think the phantom crying started early that summer, before the baby fell ill. The nights were high and fine and clear, stretching for a darkness that wouldn't fall for hours. Now the baby was in a cot, rather than the soft basket we would keep close by, I felt loose with freedom. I used the evenings to garden, to plant things and water others – and I listened to a baby crying as I did so.

This was not our baby's cry; the child was younger, it made a softer mewl, a higher pitch. It was an altogether needier noise. But I would pause and check anyway, stand still and listen. Instinctively, I knew this was not a sound I had created with my body. I thought of a newborn, hot in that early heat wave, red in the face and hungry or overtired or wanting, wanting, wanting. I thought of my son, of the calm of him sleeping. The adrenaline spike tapered off and I returned to the work between my hands, uprooting a small plant that was growing somewhere I wished it wasn't.

Those few warm weeks were marked in this way: our baby sleeping inside the house; us sitting outside it; deepening skies; me listening to another child in the neighbourhood crying. Perhaps this was when the phantom crying began. It's hard to pinpoint its genesis, this sound that existed so clearly but only inside my head, as ghostly in its origin as it is in existence. Within a moment I could dismiss the cry as a fallacy, but I nevertheless heard it. Every time I paused, allowing my body to clarify what my brain had given birth to, these babies in the head.

For a while the phantom crying stopped. We were out of the country and all sleeping in close quarters for several weeks. When we returned home the baby had grown. His cry had deepened into a throatier, more furious thing, although he made it less often. Those nights, when he would go many hours without crying, the babies returned to my head. I would put in earplugs and they would strike up: a mewling, distant chorus from my own subconscious.

I wasn't alone in this: I asked the women in my antenatal group if they heard their children crying even when they were silent, and the stories spilled forth in a flurry of messages. They heard their babies while they were in the shower or when the washing machine was on, or when someone else was holding their baby, who was quiet. Some said that in their sleep-deprived states, they'd been known to try and nurse their pillow, confusing it with their child. It reminded me of the times I had been roused from the depths of a sleep cycle by my son's cry only to start shushing him before I'd left the bed, eyes still shut, my brain making my body respond without my consciousness being aware of it.

In 1989, a story by Joyce Carol Oates was published in the *New England Review and Bread Loaf Quarterly*, a literary magazine from private liberal arts college Middlebury. The story was called 'The Crying Baby', and would appear alongside two dozen others in *Heat and Other Stories*, a collection Oates released a couple of years later. 'The Crying Baby' is told from the perspective of a 52-year-old housewife whose children have grown up and who hears a baby in the house, especially during the months when the furnace is on. It's a short story – just nine pages, a block of conversational text that could have been lifted from the pages of a diary, or a transcription from an interview – but it captures the strange reality of phantom crying; its persistence and presence, the fact a sound can be so keenly real even while you know it is false. The unnamed narrator explains the different stages of her relationship with the crying baby, from stubbornly 'begging [her family] to listen' to it, to, eventually, lying about hearing it as they begin to doubt her sanity. She tries to pinpoint when she first hears it and can't. Through her descriptions of the baby's presence we get to learn of her house and her work: 'Sometimes the sound seemed to be localized in the kitchen, sometimes in another room, upstairs or down, or in the basement, or in the attic, or in the garage adjoining the house; sometimes it began when I switched off the television set; and similarly with faucets, the vacuum cleaner, the washing machine.' We learn that the narrator's first pregnancy ended in miscarriage, that she dismisses any sentiment she may have of it, but that if she'd not had further children people would attribute her hearing a phantom baby to it, 'that discharge of mere mute tissue-dappled blood as much embarrassment as grief, and as much simple physical discomfort as either, soaked up in sanitary rags and wrapped in newspaper, bundled off with the trash'.

Still, the woman is haunted by the phantom baby, who brings 'a harsh salt mist' to her eyes. The sound exasperates her and drives her to rhetoric: 'Why do you haunt me?

Are you the infant of my house? — of the earth beneath the house? *Am I* your mother? *Is* this your womb?' In time, the woman learns to quieten the baby by singing lullabies to it, embodying her younger self as she continues with her tasks. She whispers of her menopausal life, of the 'limp and useless' womb that stands in opposition to the 'flush-cheeked giddiness of young motherhood, the tipsiness of milk-heavy breasts' that she once inhabited. Even when she is confronted by these changing states of womanhood by the presence of her daughter-in-law and infant grandson, the phantom baby is not banished. Our narrator entertains violent, destructive thoughts. She imagines herself going into the cellar to find a sledgehammer 'to smash through the very foundation of the house, every haunted fiber and nail' but realises it wouldn't offer an explanation as to why the baby was crying nor stop it. Grimly, she accepts it as a part of her being — something her children and husband will never understand, as entrenched in her as the domestic tasks that have defined her womanhood for thirty years.

Oates never had children — 'while not repulsive, [the thought of having children] simply doesn't interest me at all', she wrote in her journal — but she nevertheless captured one of the great secrets of childrearing, of what it is to have mothered even decades after birth. I found the phantom baby in my head more bemusing than anything else — irritating at 4 a.m. when everyone was asleep aside from me, admittedly, but rarely horrifying or upsetting. But I could see why Oates transforms the notion into something tormenting: a cry hard-wired to wake, distract and unnerve us that nobody else can hear is a pretty good metaphor for the isolation that certain parts of womanhood – matrescence, menopause – can bring. At one point our narrator conflates the ghostly cry with the years of invisible domestic labour she has done for her family, owning both as something only she can access: 'I have my secret knowledge, a voiceless cry intimate as the tiny bones of my inner ear or my sharp eye in its socket, regarding them with pity on *my* side, preparing their meals as I have always done, overseeing the household laid out so properly, in order, beneath the Midwestern sky, washing walls, scouring, in season ridding the eaves of hornets' nests and what all else growing like mad embroidery above our heads, amused, bemused, singing the baby to sleep when there is no danger of being overheard, no spies on the premises, all's *mine*.'

I was struck by Oates's ability to pinpoint the phantom cry, mostly because it was the most validating document I could find regarding the baby in my head. For something that was anecdotally so common, there had been seemingly little research undertaken into phantom crying. I could find a handful of studies about hearing a baby that doesn't exist, but they tended to pathologise phantom crying: it was something experienced by postnatally depressed women in Hong Kong, for instance, or as part of auditory hallucinations that happen in times of mental distress. There was research by neuroscientists that showed how parts of the brain linked to processing sound increased in size in postpartum women, but little that examines how our brains reacted to non-existent babies crying.

And yet, anecdotally at least, phantom crying appeared almost universal. There were Reddit threads with hundreds of responses attesting to the same experience ('I've bolted up out of a dead sleep before because I thought she was crying. She was totally asleep'; 'We hear our 22 month old crying even when she's at my moms house an hour away [sic]'), sometimes to the point of madness, and articles dedicated to the subject on parenting websites. Those parents who had experienced baby loss were, brutally, not immune. When I mentioned the 'fake baby' in passing on social media, I was flooded with responses from birthing parents not only knowing exactly what I meant, but also advising me that I could be hearing them for many years to come. Frustrated, I submitted a question about phantom crying to 'Wish I'd Known', an open-source website that collects data from anonymous parents on questions that slip through the cracks of the establishment. When the results came in, two-thirds of the recipients responding had experienced phantom crying. I suspected womankind had been silently listening to non-existent babies for millennia, and nobody had thought it worth researching. Like Oates's narrator, we'd been left to quieten it by ourselves, this baby that nobody else can hear.

My body was responding to things before my consciousness could be aware of them. My response to my son's cry was one of many tethers that redefined me without me realising I had become a new version of myself. My life was newly full of sounds that tore me into pieces. But sound is a being, it's an alive thing, vibrating and malleable, and if it could release such waves of change in my life then perhaps I could hear new ways of existing through it, too.

I was learning that music wasn't just confined to that recorded through complicated mixing desks or released through a radio; that the sounds I lived alongside had their own kind of song. My understanding of sound was never going to be subject to a test: I would never be able to listen to the correct number of albums, be awarded for my hearing or achieve perfect pitch. My ears had been damaged by the years I'd spent surrounding my body in music. The phantom crying I listened to, and then dismissed, most days was as real as it was ghostly. To ignore it would be to ignore my experience – and that of millions of other women like me, who had been listening and ignored for listening for generations. I'd been looking at listening – at music, at sound – as a binary when it could never be contained between two states of being. If I was going to learn how to listen more deeply I needed to shrug off the binaries of listening as either hearing — or not, of the right or wrong music and of hitting the note, or not. I was surrounded by sound that had never been notated between lines on a page, never turned into crotchets or quavers or given a musical key. This wasn't music, but it was the stuff of my life. It arguably mattered more.

Phantom crying was a global phenomenon that had been largely ignored by the scientific community, that women were never taught about in antenatal classes or given advice about by the midwife. It was both real and unreal, it existed in the amorphous, slippery and ambiguous space between the two. And it was this space that I kept being drawn to. This liminal space of sound and not-sound, of hearing and not-hearing, was increasingly appealing at a point in my life where I didn't feel seen or heard. One weekend afternoon I took the baby out and pushed the pram along the edges of a pavement filled with people a decade younger than me, spilling out of a day rave. I came out of the cornershop and bumped into them, fluffed up with excitement and substance and the anticipation of the party to come. I recognised so much of my youth in them, but I was nearly invisible; just a mum pushing a sleeping baby, in shoes they would never wear. I was neither old nor young; I didn't recognise my body, but I was fascinated by the one it had created. My days, my waking hours, were that of the in-between. Sometimes, I felt like if I were to scream nobody would hear me. No wonder I was drawn to all the things we hear that nobody has told us about.

DEEP LISTENING

We've sat in the cinema for a couple of hours now. I'm getting restless; I feel the tug between home and here particularly strongly, even though there are just a few miles between the two. I want to have an early night, to feel the physical, unspeakable comfort of knowing the bodies I love the most are within reach. The screen turns black, and white text appears. It introduces 'The Tuning Meditation', a piece by composer and musician Pauline Oliveros that was first performed in 1981 in the Guggenheim Museum. It's been recreated dozens of times since, including with a crowd of thousands at the Michigan Womyn's Music Festival. It's a classic Oliveros meditation: simple, inclusive, astounding. The instructions are straightforward:

- Breathe in and out, listening for a tone.
- On your next breath, sing the tone you have silently perceived.

- Meanwhile, listen to the voices around you, and select a tone you can hear to replicate.
- Continue by singing another tone of your own.
- Then alternate to tune into another you can hear nearby.
- Sing warmly!

As the credits roll a nervous silence bubbles up from the audience that melts with a few brave voices. Mine is among them: I hum, then open my mouth, as a mellow mid-pitched noise emerges from my throat. The woman next to me has been quietly laughing at moments during the film, just as I have been scratching a pen against the pages of a notebook. She sings too. A note a little higher, a little louder. On my right-hand side a man maintains his silence. My neighbour and I bounce off one another. I am emboldened by her voice. As I sing, I listen: a kind of harmonic chorus emerges, swelling and rising, the sounds colliding with and mimicking one another. There is no clear note or intention here beyond those we have been given, and something is happening. It feels strange and rebellious to sing in a cinema. It feels silly and delicious to sing out loud. I am having a duet with a dozen strangers. I am as conscious of the silence as I am the noise. This amorphous song rises and glows and then shrinks again, and with it my own voice. I am among the last to finish, a lone human owl hooting in the gloomy plush of a cinema seat. In the process I have been given a lived taste of Oliveros's work; of what it is to listen as much as to generate.

Screenings of *Deep Listening: The Story of Pauline Oliveros* in the UK were scant – I had gone to the nationwide premiere, along with dozens of near-identical women (glasses, tote bag, cardigan) who had chosen to spend their Saturday night watching a documentary about a dead composer who changed the way we listen. I had been gathering information about Oliveros for months. When I mentioned to people that I was interested in sound and listening, hers was the name that most consistently came up. She seemed to be one of those people who was either not heard of or thought completely brilliant: ignorance or reverence, little in between.

Oliveros died almost exactly eight years before I went to that screening. One of her final projects – one that closes the film, which was made by Daniel Weintraub during the last three years of her life and the immediate aftermath of her death – was to compose a piece to be performed in collaboration between internationally acclaimed musicians and a d/Deaf conductor. We watch as she leans over the balcony of an abandoned swimming pool in Bergen, where the performers gather, listening as these bodies connect to make a new kind of music. The list of musicians Oliveros has inspired is extensive – John Cage held her responsible for his 'finally know[ing] what harmony is' – but one of the reasons why so many non-musicians had referred me to her work was her foundation of Deep Listening. Oliveros described Deep Listening as 'a way of listening in every possible way to everything possible to hear no matter what you are doing'; what began as a concept became workshops that became a teachable practice. There are now Deep Listening workshops and retreats all over the world, based on Oliveros's theories, compositions and meditations.

The documentary offered me a crash course in Oliveros's life and career. It showed me photographs of her old-fashioned, small-town upbringing in Houston, Texas, where she picked up a variety of instruments in the school orchestra before alighting on the accordion that she'd make her lifelong favourite. She would come to let the accordion introduce itself during her performances, opening the instrument on stage before her microphone, then gently extending the bellows. Oliveros would sit back a little, close her eyes, as if she and the instrument were breathing together. It became, as her wife and collaborator IONE would describe in the introduction to Oliveros's book *Quantum Listening*, 'her trademark opening, so simple and so powerful'.

I learned that, aged 20, she left for San Francisco, where she could live openly as a gay woman and where she pursued her ambition of becoming a composer. San Francisco was formative: she was the only woman in Cline

W. Otey's composers' workshop of 25 men. I gleaned snippets of her approach — a desire to 'hear music from the inside out', to 'listen to everything all the time and remind yourself when you're not listening'. She liked, she explained in an interview, to listen to things that people usually ignore. She held the notion that the environment could become a possible orchestra, that one could turn virtually all sounds into music and that audiences could be participants, too. In time, Oliveros maintained that no expertise — musical or otherwise — was needed. That listening and sound was a means of connection. She saw the act of listening as a force of nature.

There were countless scores, experimental pieces, performances and publications. What was so apparent from the film was the sheer abundance of Oliveros's work: she made so much of it — of music, of writing, of lectures, of improvisation, of community. But to me it seemed her career existed in two halves: one academic, exclusive and patriarchal; the other a kind of expansive communality, inherently feminist and queer and with a ferociously bold intention — to position listening as a cure-all to societal ills. I wasn't a pioneering composer, and I'd not moved nearly two thousand miles to find acceptance for an existence my upbringing rejected, but this division felt familiar to me: working under the tough, armoured egotism of a newsroom, shaking it off for something less formed with a hope of freedom. I was still learning to navigate what working motherhood looked like; I was doing it on the best terms I could define for myself in that moment.

By 1970, Oliveros had started work on what she called 'Sonic Meditations', the origin and theory behind compositions like 'The Tuning Meditation' we'd been encouraged to perform in the cinema. These were Oliveros's response to the Vietnam War and the increasingly polarised society at the end of the decade — what she referred to as the 'atmosphere of war, of protest, of resistance'. Oliveros was teaching at the University of California when student George Winne Jr set himself on fire in protest to the war. Her composition, her music-making, shifted both inward and outward simultaneously: into a realm of deep introspection while expanding in terms of its accessibility and communality. She wanted the process of music-making to be something capable of healing, to have the potential to end violence. After years of being a lone woman in a tight academic enclave of composers, Oliveros started to collaborate with female sound artists and came together with the ♀ Ensemble — a women-only space for creative exploration. In the documentary about her life you can see the shift in the footage and photographs. In the first half of her career, Oliveros is surrounded by men. In the second, she keeps the company of women.

Oliveros had moved to America's east coast by the time she developed Deep Listening, the concept that has come to define her legacy. While it was certainly the culmination of her work so far – the teaching, the composition, the meditations, playing with the accordion's strange tonalities – it also arose from a pun and a place: she recorded an improvisation with two other musicians in an underground cistern. They were deep, and they were listening. In 1991 she created, with choreographer Heloise Gold and IONE, the first Deep Listening retreat. These gatherings would reverberate like sound waves: the Deep Listening Institute was founded in 2005, certifying and training Deep Listening practitioners the world over who welcome in people to listen deeply in community. 'Deep Listening puts experience before everything else,' wrote Laurie Anderson. 'It emphasizes both detail and scope of, in Pauline's words, "the sounds of daily life, of nature, of one's own thoughts".'

I keep bumping into Oliveros and her work. I think of her as a 21-year-old, hanging out of a San Francisco apartment building with her tape recorder – a birthday present from her mother – soaking up all the sounds of the world outside. I think of her instruction to listen to everything, all the time, when my world feels small and claustrophobic. When I listen, it expands. She wrote a little about babies ('the best Deep Listeners') and mothers ('listening for the least differences possible to perceive – perception at the edge of the new . . . mothers do this'), but when I looked up the Deep Listening Institute and the retreats it held it felt unfathomable for me to undertake one. I could not fly across an ocean, or even get to a meditation held on the other side of London. I never quite found the time to undertake a Sonic Meditation, even though I thought about them most days ('Take a walk at night. Walk so silently that the bottoms of your feet become ears.'). In the days after I watched the documentary about Oliveros's life, I tried to contact IONE, her wife and collaborative partner of three decades. I put out different feelers, emailed different people, but the ask sat unanswered in silence.

Oliveros wrote repeatedly about the life-long practice of listening. In the documentary those who knew her explained that she was so expert at Deep Listening that she could shift into the modality of introspection and attention it demanded seconds after cracking a joke. This was both reassuring and daunting to consider. Still, I saw the overlaps between the concept and the life I was now living. 'How we listen creates our life,' Oliveros wrote. In the depths of the night, trying to translate the cries of my child – barely louder, through the wall, than a whisper – my life had been cast anew by listening.

Oliveros's work was born of a desire for freedom – for her music, for her sexuality, for her feminism and politics, for a want of community – and that permissiveness seeps through it today. Senem Pirler, an artist, educator and musician, sought Oliveros's mentorship at the end of the composer's life. Senem had trained in a traditional conservatory as a concert pianist before becoming a sound engineer. Having Oliveros as a mentor was, she explained, 'a challenging experience at first. I had come from this idea of control: as sound engineers we are obsessed with this idea of how to polish things, how to make sound perfect and control the environment. When I started to work with [Oliveros] I started to question that: what is this idea of controlling something?'

Deep Listening is, Senem explained in a podcast interview, 'a very messy practice. You don't get to do it perfectly all the time, because it's basically all about awareness . . . it's about being comfortable with the chaos and actually finding creative moments in the chaos that comes to you.' Part of the reason why it felt daunting to embark on a Deep Listening practice was because creating the space and time to develop attention and awareness felt impossible: my mind was eternally distracted, by the baby or the conversation I was trying to have or my phone or the endless cycle of tidying and sorting and cleaning that had somehow become my life. But at the same time I was emitting a new radar of focus in a way I'd not felt before, a new way of listening: to the roar of an approaching motorbike when I tried to cross the road with the pushchair, to a friend as I assessed what my son was putting in his mouth, to the phantom babies and the mental maths around a nap schedule in my head. As Senem spoke about the challenge Deep Listening posed to her quest for perfect sound, I realised that was part of the practice: I was unlikely to walk into a space dedicated to Deep Listening, slip off my shoes and begin perfectly participating any time soon. But I could – and I was – folding a greater awareness of how I listened into my daily life. If how we listen creates our life, I was undeniably creating something.

WHITE NOISE

As spring gave way and the phantom crying arrived, my hearing otherwise began to fade. Neither completely nor permanently, but enough to conjure a different kind of existence for a few days. The end of my fourth trimester arrived and with it a pressure inside my ears that I haven't felt since childhood, when I was besieged with ear infections. Sound became sharp and woozy. The doctor said my ear canals were tiny and blocked, and I left the baby with my husband to have them cleared in an uncomfortable ricochet of squeaking and loud air that made sound newly precise.

Months later, I caught Covid and it left me fuzzy. I felt as if I was constantly bumping through a new realm of high pressure without being able to readjust. Sound became noise, and that noise was both far away and ever-present. To sit around a table of friends in a pub was a kind of sensory overload, with the voices of those I wanted to hear blending amorphously with the clattering of the kitchen and the background hubbub bouncing off the hardwood floor. The constant hum of traffic, usually so easily tuned out, became amplified to an ever-present white noise whenever I left the house. Other people's words became dim and difficult to hear. I was newly conscious of shouting, not being able to hear myself speak properly, and so dialled myself down just in case.

At the time, the baby and I were still waking in the night, our bodies separated by a wall and doors but nevertheless twinned. When I woke up in the minutes before he did, it was quiet enough for the strangeness of my altered hearing to take on a new guise. With my ears muffled by the pillow I could connect to the new box of sound that had replaced the hearing clarity I'd been fortunate to take for granted. This twilight silence was deep enough for me to tune in. I heard my heartbeat, the unmistakable pulse of blood pushing through the capillaries in my head. By day my ears had become a constant irritant, but I could now appreciate their new, altered state. I wondered if this was what it sounded like to be in the womb.

An onslaught of low-level illness arrived in the house, the kind of thing new parents are warned about as their babies grow. I found a new resilience, a meagre kind of persistence in a body that would previously have taken a day off work. We muddled through, taking temperatures and wiping a small nose. I learned to calm myself when the too-loud sound of the baby's racking cough pierced through my awareness and raised my adrenaline. Over these weeks, these months, I tuned into my hearing, and it was worsening. The distant ringing and traffic-like hum of my tinnitus grew louder when I was ill. Among activity and other noise, it was usually ignorable: I was distracted by the demands of my son, of the housework, of the places we had to be and the people we were meeting. If I had once been familiar with the noises of the city – of the warning beep that precedes the unforgiving swoosh of closing Tube carriage doors – my day was now soundtracked by the music of my motherhood. The rhythmic gurgle of the washing machine, the same saccharine songs about recycling made by my son's toy truck, the recorded reminder to 'please stay with your buggy for your child's safety' that followed me down the aisle of the bus. As the baby grew, I would feel confident enough to leave him for a minute or two, listening out for evidence of his safety: the banging of wooden blocks or the shaking of a rattle, the happy squawk that accompanied discovering a door to open or a drawer to empty. These were the noises that would echo back my one-sided conversations, of explaining to him how we would eat lunch, and what we would eat, and how then it would be time for his nap. Breaking down the hours into endless, tiny, mind-numbing realities. Some days it felt like listening to a scratched record that got stuck in the same broken groove. Some days it felt like a contentment I could never have imagined.

My acknowledgement of these sounds – of the kitchen, of the whistling and the pulsing of blood in my ears – was new. Nearly two years earlier, standing in the warm wooden cavern of the Integratron, I had understood my life to be something quiet that needed noise to be pressed upon it, like fingers into wet clay. Now I'd learned that my life was filled with sound, albeit of a nature that I'd not previously considered valid. I sang to my son daily, usually because it somehow took less effort than speaking to him. Most weeks I would sing in a circle of other women with small children. We'd learn and recall the lyrics and melodies to songs about mice running up clocks and crocodiles swimming down rivers. Sitting on the scratchy, institutional carpets of libraries and children's centres we would clap and move our bodies, release our voices in a kind of unison. In the Mojave Desert I'd felt on the shift of something, outgrowing a life I wasn't entirely ready to leave yet, entering one that felt too big for me. I wasn't to know that within two months of being there I'd be facing the entire other precipice of pregnancy. At the time I was beginning to mourn what music had been for me, the grip it held on me. I'd not been to a club or a gig in months; even the memories of it felt like a faint echo.

And yet, the basic actions were the same. I sang among

strangers, I raised my hands in the air, I came together in communion with people I didn't know all sharing the experience of belting out the words. This music, this experience, though, is considered less than. Less skilled, less virtuosic, less likely to deliver transcendence. People do not queue up for rhyme time as they would for a nightclub, nor make annual pilgrimages for another round of 'Hop Little Bunnies' as they might for Glastonbury. It feels borderline preposterous to point this out. One is so upheld, so lauded, so aspirational. I have contributed to this through years of music journalism, of romanticising what it is to stand among strangers and bear witness to musicians – some god-like in their talent, many others just people doing a job – creating things that are alive and extraordinary and ripe with meaning. The other is dismissed, made invisible and infantilised. But both are doing the same work: making music, bringing people together, communicating through song. One is a world dominated by men. The other by women.

Before the baby was born my sister advised me that having a child was not unlike going to Glastonbury. In the weeks after, I understood deeply what she meant. Both involve sleepless nights and body fluids. Both require a certain physical stamina, often on poor nutrition and some dehydration. There are moments, during both, when it is tiring, and the adrenaline and endorphins wear off and you wonder why you're doing it, so low is the mood and the energy. Both endure because they offer moments of dizzying, freewheeling euphoria. I have never felt the edges of my humanity quite so keenly during those first aching, bloodied and raw weeks of my matrescence. I have never felt so brutally, beautifully alive than at Glastonbury Festival. The difference is that one lasts for less than a week, and the other changes a person for ever.

Because my life was made of a kind of music. Not just in the nursery rhymes but in the noises made by my child; in the consoling, connecting voice notes sent to me by friends, some of them also mothering; in the conversations that would strike up on public transport, London's froideur melting away in the blink of my son's blue eyes. With time I was learning to recognise a kind of music in my haphazard hearing, too. To recognise the beats and the burbles that interrupted the silence of the dead of night as the sounds of my lived experience, rather than an impediment to them. Increasingly, I was seeing the two as being connected: neither of these soundscapes would be formally identified as music, but they existed and they comprised a significant part of my reality. How to chart on a score noises that only you can hear, or make a symphony from the sound a baby makes when he learns he can climb the stairs?

When artist Christine Sun Kim undertook a residency at Somerset House, a flag was hoisted above the London building's grand courtyard. It was white, with a spidery score on it. Kim creates and refers to musical notation a lot in her work, and the flag that flew above London bore a score for a song that had been devised by her daughter. It was called 'A Song About A Family' and was captured in a mixture of invented, if recognisable, musical notation interspersed with drawings of hearts. Only Kim's daughter would know what her composition originally sounded like, but the invitation was clear: every passer-by was welcome to read — and play — the music, to interpret it as we wished.

When I thought about the noise of my home, the noise of my matrescence, I thought about the score created by Christine Sun Kim's daughter and how Kim had hung it above London. I'd been ignoring these domestic scores, I think, for the same reason that a lot of realities are ignored: they are considered of little to no value within patriarchal, late capitalist, Western society. In speaking with women who listened differently, with their bodies or with devoted intention, who listened within the world of noise left behind by traumatic birth or a deep-rooted survival instinct laid deep within our humanity, I was beginning to tune into a whole new spectrum of sound. I also started to listen differently.

These new interpretations were quiet, still. They were quiet and they were sometimes inaudible, as varying and incomprehensible as the whomping bassline in my head or the babbling of my child. But they were undeniably there: whispers. Whispers are synonymous with gossip and fallacy, but they're also the beginnings of change and revolution. Among marginalised people whispers can become lifelines. Whispers are what brave people make when they aren't given the room to speak. Whispers are easily dismissed and made to be denied; they can take as much courage to believe as to make. And when whispers become networks – often built by women – they begin to erode power: they pass on warnings and survival strategies. They are difficult to substantiate because to be deniable is the only way they can be passed on.

Now that I'd encountered these different experiences of listening, I wanted to understand them and I wanted to hear more. To do so, I would need to challenge the privileges that had guided my listening so far. I would need to encounter – and learn from – women who listened in wholly different ways and realms than I had experienced.

July

WE TAKE HIM TO THE HOSPITAL on a Monday night. It's a sudden decision, in the end, after a day of thinking such measures unnecessary. The baby is hot, he's been hot all day, but now he is scalding, and his skin is red and he won't stop making a strange, high little cry. We order a cab and gather our things so quickly it's only later, hours later, that we realise we're wearing matching striped jumpers, like mimes. In the car I start to silently cry. I look out the window to distract myself and the sky is striped beautifully with pink. As we get the pram out of the boot the taxi driver says, kindly, 'He'll be all right.' I still think back on that moment.

We're seen swiftly, even though I can't say much more than 'My baby is three months old, and he has a temperature' at reception. Ushered through into the serious bit of paediatric A&E, where it's impossible to know who else they're looking after or what the time is. Hours pass and he's still crying and in hindsight I realise I'm in denial about it, that I think it's normal for him to be awake and inconsolable at two in the morning. In time the doctor will finish her shift, but not before saying that in bringing him in when we did, we saved his life. It's meant to make us feel better, I think, but I hold on to that phrase and her repetition of it like a clip from a horror film on replay for the rest of the year.

The first time they cannulate him I'm scooped up by a ward sister who types very hard and very fast. She fills a flimsy plastic cup with ice cold water and sits me down next to her desk while she hits the plastic keys with her fingers. The tapping is almost enough to drown out his screams. In memory, it is all the roaring white noise of adrenaline, the hard, futile scrunch of a paper towel against my cheeks and her furious typing. When they come to lumbar puncture him they suggest we leave the room and instead I leave the hospital entirely. It's nearly dawn now, the sky a flat grey just before it turns to daybreak. We walk back into the hospital a few minutes later and even through multiple doors I swear I can hear him. I linger in this strange in-between, knowing I can't go to him. Two parents without a baby by a reception desk. We walk back into the ward and he is in the arms of a nurse. He is still, his face salt-licked. He seems deflated, almost, by what he's been through.

I soon learn that I can't be in the room when they

pierce his skin, because bearing witness to his pain dissolves me. I become animalistic, I melt, my vision blurs with tears even while the scenes etch themselves in my memory. Usually my husband is with the baby but sometimes, during the nights, he is not. And so I walk out the door as the medics prepare their sharp little instruments, feeling like I am betraying him, that I am failing him as a mother, all the while knowing that if I stay, I won't cope.

Blood tests and cannulation must happen repeatedly over the days we spend in and return to hospital, and when they do I retreat to the corridor, feeling out of place as I try and fail to escape his cries. I am a woman in a paediatric ward with no child to hold, no noodles to heat up, no book under her arm. These stretches of time feel endless. In reality they last less than ten minutes.

There are many sounds in a hospital and those who work there are used to them. I know of medics who have preferred to labour in a hospital ward because they find comfort in the machines and the numbers and the quiet cacophony of bleeps. Every machine has its own song; some hum and others emit polyphonic ditties. When my baby's heart rate and temperature spike, the machines glow red and let out a wailing siren. I can't convince the staff to attend to him because these noises have become background murmurs to them. I sit and watch the numbers teeter, as if they might lower if I stare hard enough. I feel the panic register in my blood. I can't stop this unbidden orchestra. He lies there, asleep, immune to the noise while the infection charges around his body.

After a few days, I learn more about the machines. I learn which button to press to turn the sound off. I have not slept for more than 40 minutes at a time, a handful of times a day. I am sustained by the salty softness of hospital food, adrenaline and fierce love for my son. I exist in a state of high, barbed alert. These bleeps punctuate the empty waiting of the hours. I hear other children – older children, sicker children – crying, but I can't see them. Their sound is not made by my son, and while they are upsetting, they do not turn my body into an alarm.

When it is time for another procedure, I leave my baby and pace the corridors. I take in the attempts to brighten up the place – the poster-paint handprints and the laminated pictures of cartoon characters. A baby bouncer lies folded and inert atop a filing cabinet. It is late but the fluorescent lighting maintains a state of permanent, sickly illumination. I hear other children, the chirruping of television on iPads, and then his wail begins. I know its parabolic pattern by now. I am over 30 metres away and yet it bores into me. It's quiet, technically. Quieter than the squeak of a door hinge or the footsteps of a nurse, but as it ratchets up in pitch and volume my blood pumps fast and thick through my veins; I feel it pulsing between my ribs. This is a cry into the ether that is destined for my reaction, that I would recognise anywhere. This is a sonar between us. I imagine it like concentric circles on the navigation deck of a boat. I imagine it as something physical, as if I were a bat or a whale, dependent on it for navigation.

I find a room where I cannot hear him and the quiet is uneasy. There are other mothers in here, heating up food in the microwave, catching a breath with other adults who are not medical staff. The sounds here are simple, almost to the point of domesticity, but it is no haven. In the absence of my son's sound I can't know that he is breathing. It is as if he has vanished with his cry. And so I drift back into the corridor, to walk it, listening, until I can hear him again. The cries wind down, as if batteries are running out. I see a glimpse of my husband's shoe through the glass pane of the door. The doctor comes out. I am full of hope and relief, but they haven't managed to cannulate. 'His hands are covered in puncture wounds,' she tells me. I reply that he has had five cannulas inserted and fail in the past three days.

This will keep happening for a while yet. We return the next day; my husband goes in with the baby and a registrar who carries the air of experience. I stand in the family room. The nurse on the desk asks me if that is my baby crying. When he is well enough for us to finally return home the softness of it all after days of clinical linoleum feels like a dampener. I am wild with relief and a new, heightened sense of danger. I will come to think of the woman I was before all this as a totally different, wholly naive, blissfully ignorant kind of mother. At times, I will think I hate her.

My life shrinks. I empty my calendar out like a shopping bag. Sometimes, we interrupt our day with a baby class and I pretend that everything is back to normal. I am so tired that I feel as if I exist in a twilight space separate to the daily life that everyone else inhabits. Once I have put the baby down for a nap and tidied the kitchen and remembered to eat, I try to sleep myself, but he wakes up 15 minutes later. The hours stretch and warp.

I crave the life I used to have. I want to be the mother I insisted I would be, the one who could leave her husband to put the baby to bed and go out with her friends, not blurred into something removed from the world. I text a friend and tell her we should go for cocktails; I shrug off the clothes I have been wearing for days and put on make-up. I leave the house as the baby screams at his bottle and make the adrenaline of it take me underground, where all the other people are going about their business, ripe with summer and commuting and evening plans. I stare at people standing outside a pub in their shirtsleeves like they are a museum exhibit. We order food. We order drinks. We talk about my friend's work and the holidays we have planned and the new friends I have made through having a baby. We do not talk about the baby's illness, although it is all I can think about. We walk past people drinking and dating and into a basement where cocktails are served at tables from little brown paper menus and I order something French and chic and I don't look at my phone; there isn't a signal in here anyway.

When I emerge, it feels too early to be going home, but it is nevertheless too late. The baby has woken up and won't settle. I have missed texts and calls from my husband, who is coping, but wants to know when I will be back; there is not enough milk expressed to sate the baby. It will take me 40 minutes to get home and it feels like a lifetime. The papery facade I have been wearing crumples. I retrace my way across the city, underground, on the Tube, out again. Matt has left me a voicemail by accident and it is minutes of my hungry, unsettled, recovering child crying. I listen to it as I wait for a bus and, when it doesn't come immediately, frantically try to hail a cab. I am terrorised by the sound of it. I can't believe I have done this; I can't believe I was stupid enough to think I could leave him. I am another person now, another woman now, one that is made of fragments.

VIBRATIONS

Pushing myself into realms of silence had shown me that an absence of sound was more complicated than I'd envisaged. Speaking to Claire and Jane had shown me a small part of all the ways that people can understand noise and how they listen to it. The struggles I had to hear as a child had evolved into a tinnitus that made my experience of sound unwittingly unique to my understanding of the world. I am a hearing person living in a world created by hearing people, but many others experience sound and music from a non-hearing perspective. For decades society has ignored and othered the d/Deaf community, who have been bombarded with 'cures' and treatments to improve their hearing to achieve a kind of acceptable conformity. 'Deafness is revealed only when engaged in conversation with a deaf person or a group of signers,' writes Jaipreet Virdi in *Hearing Happiness*, a book that explores the author's experience of deafness alongside the history of deafness cures. 'Yet deafness has no meaning other than what is assigned to it, meanings created by hearing people projecting their own ideals of hearing and normality, or even meanings ascribed by deaf persons themselves.' People who are d/Deaf or hard of hearing listen in ways that the non-disabled and hearing people of the world rarely take time to consider, often, in the rush to 'fix' d/Deaf people, ignoring what a lived experience of deafness might be. We're so quick to project a means and expectation of sensory experience upon others that we don't make any space to actually understand what the world sounds like to them first.

I was interested in the idea of Deaf Gain, a term created by artist Aaron Williamson in 1998, who asked why 'hearing loss and not gaining deafness?'. For those people who were born d/Deaf, some would argue that they've not lost hearing – they just didn't have it in the first place. Among a society of people who understand the world without sound, not hearing things doesn't matter. But in the hearing world, where sound does matter – where it matters so much it becomes, argues artist Christine Sun Kim, who is deaf, equal to 'money, power, control – social currency' – d/Deaf people's experience of sound can create new means of understanding and communication, regardless of the language a person speaks. Kim's work navigates the role that sound plays in society, through drawings, paintings, video work and by playing with and challenging oral languages. Her TED talk, 'The enchanting music of sign language', which compares music and American Sign Language – and makes a compelling argument for hearing people to learn it – as well as retelling the history of her artistic practice, has been viewed over two million times. 'I actually know sound,' Kim says during the talk. 'I know it so well that it doesn't have to be something that's just experienced through the ears. It could be felt tactually, or experienced as a visual, or even as an idea. So I decided to reclaim ownership of sound and to put it into my art practice.' Her work began to get bigger in scale. In 2019 she covered a London billboard hundreds of metres long with the words: **IF SIGN LANGUAGE WAS CONSIDERED EQUAL, WE'D ALREADY BE FRIENDS**. Two years later she applied closed captions to the entire city of Manchester: **[THE SOUND OF SEARCHING FOR SEATING]** spanned the side of Selfridges; **[THE SOUND OF NO OTHER CITY]** crept up the lift shaft of the Ducie Street Warehouse; **[THE SOUND OF PATTING YOURSELF ON THE BACK FOR BEING ON TIME]** sat atop the entrance to Manchester Piccadilly station. 'Doing all that work has given me the realisation that scale equals visibility,' she said in an interview a few years later. 'And that has the ability to shape social norms. I want deaf lives to be in your mind and be part of what we consider acceptable, what's normal. If you don't see us, we have no place to be.' If I wanted to understand how sound had shaped my life, how it had impacted my understanding of the world and the people I encountered in it, I needed to explore what it was to listen without taking sound for granted.

It sounds different in the theatre. I have rushed to be here, run up the escalators in the station and over the cobbled streets beyond. The show will start shortly and I don't want to be denied entry for being too late. As I apologetically make my way past a row of knees, I realise that it is both quieter than usual and more atmospheric. A man in the front row is standing up and signing to someone sitting at the back of the stalls. The woman sitting next to me is wearing hearing aids. In the row in front, two people are flicking through large-print programme notes. I am among an audience of people who are communicating using their hands and faces and bodies; I can't understand BSL, but I am aware of the anticipatory hubbub that is rising from the seats around me nevertheless. A flutter of hands, laughter, people catching up before curtain up.

I'm here to see *Self-Raising*, a show co-written and performed by Jenny Sealey, who has been the artistic director of Graeae (pronounced 'grey–eye'), the UK's flagship disability-led theatre company, since 1997 and co-directed the opening ceremony of the 2012 Paralympic Games. Jenny was born hearing but became deaf after a childhood accident. She's in her early sixties now, and appears on stage with her 'terp', or interpreter, beneath a large screen upon which family photographs and captions based on Jenny's script are projected. Jonah, her 29-year-old video director son, is behind us, keeping the captions on the screen. It is his voice that some people in the crowd can hear when the photographs are described during the show. Jenny has dedicated her career to improving inclusion and accessibility for d/Deaf, blind and disabled people in theatre – both on stage and off. Like many of the shows she has made, *Self-Raising* is fully accessible.

I meet Jenny a couple of weeks before I go to see *Self-Raising*, in an empty boardroom of Graeae's offices. As we speak, she notices, with excitement, that her set for *Self-Raising* is being wheeled in. I had wanted to speak to Jenny not just because she is deaf, but because she is a pioneer in an industry where listening is crucial. Actors and directors listen out for meaning in the script, to the other performers and creatives working alongside them and to the audience. Even if you know your lines, the way another cast member speaks a line on stage can vary from one performance to another; an actor must listen to that and respond accordingly. If actors didn't listen to one another, they would say their lines at the wrong time or fail to react when the fake gunshot rises into the air. But beyond practicalities, to perform is to listen in a way of existing in that moment alone, of listening, re-listening and responding every time. This is the case for actors from the d/Deaf community too, but with a crucial difference: they can't hear.

I open our interview by asking Jenny what listening means to her. The question reverberates through our conversation, and it's clear that Jenny is thinking about it — as a sense, as a word, as the role it has played in her life. Her deafness doesn't stop her from having tinnitus, nor from having the tune of 'The First Noel' currently stuck in her head. Even now, even after all her work, she is challenged when she tells the singers and musicians she's working with that she will be giving them directorial notes. When she's directing a musical, she will go through the music with a hearing person, so she can understand how the words and the rhythm fit together. 'When the actors are on stage, if I pull them up on something, they'll say: "But you can't hear me." But I can see — I can see that the lights have gone out of your eyes, I could see that your body posture was slightly different, that you're not being authentic.' Jenny hears notes beyond the music — those of the 'physical, emotional visibility of how you are when you connect with that note'.

The notion of listening acts as a guide to the stories Jenny tells me about how she has lived and worked. What she says is fascinating: as *Self-Raising* attests, Jenny has navigated her own way through a life that has been vivid and revolutionary and loud — even if her experience of it has at times existed between silence and noise. The medical establishment advised Jenny's parents not to teach her BSL, and she was treated no differently from her three hearing sisters at home. Her school ignored her deafness to the extent that when she read the words 'hard of hearing' on a noticeboard in secondary school she interpreted it as suggesting she was in some way responsible for her deafness, that 'maybe I'm not trying hard enough to hear'. She was shouted at by audiologists – as a child, when they were trying to understand the limits of her hearing and by the clinic receptionists in adulthood when she didn't hear them calling her name in the waiting room – and, with another pupil who had hearing problems, left behind to record radio programmes for their teacher when the rest of the class went swimming, which they were excluded from. ('We just knew what time it had started and had to pray to dear God it was on the right station. Once we recorded a programme about sex by mistake.')

It was Jenny's dance teacher, Miss Morrison, who gave her the beginnings of an education in physicality and rhythm that would come to define her life and the work she has done at Graeae. 'She said, "It's not an issue, it doesn't matter about the music or if you can't hear. Dancing is in the body." With her help, I taught myself to have a really good internal rhythm and a sense of musicality for which I am eternally grateful. It has served all my life as an actor, as a director and as a person. Because we did ballet, we did competitions and we did shows using our bodies to tell stories. That showed me how you could tell a story with no words.' By the time she was at university Jenny had taught herself the systems needed to act on stage. 'Every d/Deaf actor I know learns all the script, and they learn the internal rhythm of a line. So they know if someone's finished theirs,' she explains. But the university she had applied to wouldn't let her on the drama course because 'they were worried about if I'd hear the cues'.

This attitude pervaded for years. 'When I first started out at Graeae a lot of the drama schools would say, "What's the point of us teaching d/Deaf and disabled people? There aren't any jobs for them." And there's not enough books written about disability, or with disabled characters. I said, "Well, actually, we are part of the fabric of society, as parents, as mothers, as lovers, as siblings, as workers. Come on."' Things have started to shift, she says, in the past 15 to 20 years – although progress in representation is slow. Graeae has created the notion of 'the aesthetics of access' – building accessibility into performance, rather than leaving it to be an optional afterthought. When the company was awarded for its promotion of diversity at the National Theatre Awards, Jenny got up on stage and explained they'd won 'because we work with the people that none of you will'.

A lot of the company's work involves training actors with access requirements to work together, something that involves raw ingenuity on a case-by-case basis. In the process, hearing actors learn from the physicality that d/Deaf actors come to rely upon, developing cues and new patterns of understanding: 'So no hearing person ever forgets their cue towards me. Hearing and d/Deaf actors, it becomes really beautifully tightly woven by the musicality and the cueing of action.' There was one play, Jenny tells me, where a d/Deaf BSL user and a blind person were cast in roles that sat very closely together. 'I paired them together because they were the best people for that role, and that's what we do: we cast the best people,' Jenny explains. It was only later, when the actors came together, that it became apparent that Margo, who is blind, couldn't see what Steven, who is d/Deaf, was signing, and he couldn't lip-read what she was saying. Jenny asked if Margo could feel Steven's breath: 'Because if you can get really in tune with his signing, that becomes your rhythm and your beats – if you really, really listen.' She instructed Steven to look really closely at Margo's mannerisms. 'We found a physicality, the visuals, and the aurals,' Jenny says. 'But both of them had to learn every beat of the play. We did it. It was hard, but it is possible. And I think that's what I love, finding those possibilities.'

Still, 'listening' is a word that scares Jenny, tugs her back to that sudden childhood silence that she was left to navigate for herself. 'It's the hardest word, "listen",' she says, quietly. Jenny explains it takes her back to her mother, to all the times she got in trouble because of something she couldn't hear, to the hours of missed conversations when people turned their head away, so she couldn't lip-read. Listening is, she says, 'about using my eyes', although she rejects the 'myth' that d/Deaf people 'over-compensate with their eyes'. 'I guess I listen with all of me,' she says. 'I listen with my eyes and my body, not so much my ears.' And so, listening to her body has become 'really important'; her hearing was 'absolutely askew' when she went through the menopause, for instance. 'Your body is a musical instrument and it will tell you things,' she says. 'You need to be aware, you need to listen in. And I'm really good at that.' In teaching herself to lip-read – in teaching herself how to cope without verbal communication – she has learned to listen more deeply. It's something she passes on when groups from corporate offices come into Graeae to learn how to improve their communication skills: 'I ask them to look at who's in the room and they find it really hard, they're so used to being on their phone. I can listen to people because I've had to work out what the conversation has been visually. Body language is extraordinary.' As Jenny will tell us later on stage during *Self-Raising*, 'I love people's faces.'

In a society more accommodating of deafness, Jenny wouldn't have been left to cope with her sudden deafness as a child. If sign language was considered equal, we'd already be friends. Recent shifts in government policy have introduced BSL as a language to learn at GCSE, d/Deaf contestants have appeared on *Strictly Come Dancing* and *Gladiators*, and d/Deaf characters and storylines have appeared in popular shows such as *Bridgerton* and *Sex Education*, but d/Deaf culture is still far from mainstream. The majority of us have never had to question our hearing or imagine a world where sound has a different existence; what we don't realise is how our bodies, identities and communities might change if we did. The aesthetics of access may have grown from a practical need to cope with an existence where sound is absent or heard less, but in creating it Graeae also introduced hearing and non-disabled people to new means of expression. When we embrace other ways of listening, we all benefit.

To listen differently sometimes means to exist differently, and when we exist differently, our identity can change in the process. The notion of motherhood I'd drawn up before I'd given birth was rapidly becoming a fantasy, because for all the thinking I'd done about whether to have a child or not, I'd not really acknowledged what motherhood might be like. Society doesn't make space for mothers to be listened to, let alone accommodated or embraced. I was having to form a whole new identity — through listening to other women, yes, but also from learning to not listen to things beyond them that weren't helpful. I was feeling my way, picking up wisdom from the more experienced mothers who were patient and generous with their knowledge, but also navigating the stop-start vibrations of living in a changed state.

For sound artist Jané Mackenzie, coming to acknowledge and embody her identity as what she defines as a 'deaf or hard of hearing person' was crucial to making sense of a childhood where her deafness wasn't entirely accommodated. Her deafness is hereditary: her mother and aunts are also deaf, but growing up in the Scottish Highlands in the Nineties, Jané says, meant that while she was surrounded by deaf women, deafness wasn't necessarily accommodated. She wore hearing aids as a child, but she was part of the first generation in her family to do so: the women in the generation above her didn't wear hearing aids until middle age. 'There was no option of sign language,' she says, 'because if you don't have someone showing you those examples, the same with wearing a hearing aid, and in our family, they didn't . . . We never talked about being deaf, it was just this dynamic of our family.'

Jané and I happen to be local; I'd encountered her work online and asked if she'd meet me so we could speak about it, and so we do in a nearby cafe. Jané is tall and angular; high cheekbones, short fringe; she wears a lime-green jumper and chunky silver jewellery hangs around her neck and from her ears, stark against her dark hair. This city has held Jané for over a decade now. 'I still have a bit of a fear about how quiet the Highlands is when

I'm back home,' she tells me, adding that as a child she would stay with her aunt, who lived in a city in Northern Ireland. 'I remember just feeling so much calmer when I did hear noise and cars and things like that. There's still something quite comforting about the noises of the city.' It's a noise she says she can choose to tune in and out of, 'because I can take my hearing aids out'.

The Highlands and her deafness have changed for Jané while she's lived in London. The tacit acceptance of deafness at home meant that she 'never found it really, like, an issue', but nevertheless had to develop her own methods of existing in a hearing world. 'For most of my life being deaf was a hidden thing that got exposed sometimes. Sometimes I chose when it got exposed and sometimes I didn't. And sometimes when it was exposed it was really painful.' Someone offered to pray for her to 'heal' her deafness. 'Of all the things I would ask for someone to pray for, that is not among them,' she laughs. 'It did feel like a bit of a shame thing.'

'You develop strategies,' Jané says. 'My friend at school would just tell me what the teacher said; I learned a lot from reading. I think if you don't meet many people who are d/Deaf, or it's not that well-known, they ask if you miss social cues or things like that. Reflecting back on my life, I can recall some strange moments. I remember being in a tent as a teenager, camping, and not being able to follow conversation. I guess in retrospect there are painful aspects. But is that more painful than any other teen experience? I don't know. Maybe I have missed social cues. But also I think it heightens things, you look for other social cues. Like you just learn a different way of understanding social cues. And maybe because I'm neurodivergent it's also that there's a bit of an overlap.'

In her twenties, after a lifetime of 'aligning [herself] to a hearing world', Jané started to engage with Deaf culture through her practice as an artist. 'The thing that has helped me most is the community side of it: Deaf culture and Deaf experience.' In recent years, Jané's practice has seen her create workshops and spaces that enable participants – many of them Deaf and neuroqueering, a verb given to the practice of subverting, defying or disrupting the heteronormative and neuronormative constructs that uphold society – to share their experience in an accessible way. In one workshop, Jané encouraged her participants to bring along a sound object. 'Someone brought a massive bottle of water, someone brought like a midi DJ controller thing from Japan, someone brought a video game, someone brought a vibration vest. I brought a broken TV. We put them all in the middle and it just became this, like, sound exchange. It was a really nice way for people to connect and get to know each other in a wordless way.' These rooms held the potential for new ways of listening, because they enabled people to do so in multi-sensory ways: 'Because we took a really robust way of listening, it allowed us to have all of our experiences be valid, whereas maybe in the dominant setting of something being this perfect note, it would shut down a lot of our personal experiences.'

Jané embarked on the workshops partially to question her concept of total sound, which had been inspired by the notion of total communication — that 'empathy, dancing, movement are valid forms of communication. I wanted to do that with sound,' she explains. 'So sound not just as something you hear, but something you may experience. It was the question of total sound. What does total sound mean? What might total sound for Deaf and neurodivergent people be?'

In the process, total sound became a question for Jané herself. She developed the concept of E land, named after her own corruption of *eilean*, the Gaelic word for the islands she grew up looking out at in near-silence. E land is an 'imagining of a place for Deaf and neuroqueer experience of sound'. Jané says she found parallels between Deaf and neuroqueer culture and how Gaelic culture related to the landscape; spending time sitting on the rocks where she grew up, looking out to sea, she learned more about her experience of herself in relation to her surroundings: 'The sea, light and colours that fascinate me like a friend you never tire of.' Crucially, E Land is not a definite destination so much as something constantly evolving and shifting, not unlike the movement of tides against islands, or light upon water, themselves. 'There wasn't a conclusion,' she tells me. 'Like, there's not a nice definition of what total sound is. But this is my experience.'

E Land is the product of coming up against different kinds of accessibility when planning workshops for people with different needs, and collaborating with other artists who see, hear and experience the world differently. It's a place established through the experience of attending queer and d/Deaf raves, places where society is rendered anew because it's easier to communicate through dancing than it is through speech. Jané talks about being a support worker for a young boy who had a neurological condition which significantly affected his hearing and sight. Going for walks with him, she says, was 'the most fun, because he would just put his hands on everything, he experienced London in a total way. People would ask me, "How do you communicate with him?" But he showed me his world in so many different ways.' The boy's favourite toy, she says, was a broken television that played the same DVD on repeat, the screen holding ever-changing bright colours as nursery rhymes played. 'He'd hug it and lick it and keep playing it,' she recalls. 'He just exuded sensory beingness. I found that really liberating and awakening. He taught me a lot.'

Engaging with Deaf culture has brought Jané a freedom and reclamation of the parts of the world that were kept at a distance for much of her life. 'I've looked at [being deaf] from all these different angles and actually it's been celebratory, like a spiritual connection. When you're hiding something, it dampens you a bit. It would be a lie to say that I'm always really comfortable telling someone I'm deaf; it's not something that's always comfortable. I can't lie about that. But I mean, when I don't have to hide it means I can be more free to talk about my own experience of sound or be drawn to spaces. Do these collaborations. Be more comfortable to take up space around these things.'

Through this work — the workshops, being a support worker, engaging with her community — Jané has come to redefine listening for herself. Originally trained as a visual artist, she now sees sound as her medium; Jané has come to reclaim sound after a childhood of feeling excluded from it. After spending her life trying to adjust her listening to a world that didn't share her lived experience, Jané's realised that when the parameters are shifted, everyone hears more.

It's still early when we leave the cafe, and we say goodbye in a reversal of how we started: I unlock the bike, the HGVs rattle past before I merge onto the tarmac among them. As I cycle, senses automatically keying into the traffic after years of pushing pedals along this same stretch of road, I see that my understanding has shifted in the space of a morning. I'm struck by Jané's journey, how her world has opened up from childhood, expanded into entire new realms. How it's still expanding, how she's still exploring it. I look at the familiarities of my neighbourhood and I think about the boy she worked with, how I would experience these landmarks if I encountered the world the way that he did. From my limited lived experience of deafness, from my far greater experience of being a hearing person, I had swallowed the misunderstanding that being without sound was to suffer. I hadn't realised that it could, instead, offer a radically different way of listening.

A few days later Jané emails me. 'Much of what I like about making art is the focus on being less verbal/spoken, so I wanted to share some written words/links I've made since we chatted, as often these things sit with me,' it opens. I bump into the ease with which I've let my privilege guide our interaction: I like to do interviews in person, conversationally, with a recorder on the table. 'As always,' Jané reminds me before she continues, 'these things are evolving.'

The email is long and generous, an additional blanket of depth and thinking over the subjects we discussed when we met. I am aware that, for a conversation about listening and experiencing sound, we didn't speak that deeply on what sound is to Jané, something she writes about. 'I love sound's innate resistant quality, how it engulfs and changes the environment. Its ability to elude and transcend spoken word to communicate and congregate. Playing with sound's social, physical and visual dimensions has been a surprising solace; exploring the contextual and sensory origins of a composition, less about a final outcome and more like a conversation.' She writes about the realm of understanding, how British Sign Language — something she has been learning as an adult, having not been exposed to it as a child — differs depending on context, much like Gaelic, and her determination to 'dissolve the ideas of a singular understanding and experience. It is not about a set output or some expertise, but more positioning myself for discovery as a means of being.'

This unlocks something for me. Speaking with, and hearing from, Jané has made me understand that I had set up impossible parameters — or certainly ones that funnelled something as broad and expansive as a sense into a narrow destination. I had set myself the challenge of 'listening more deeply' as if there would be an end point to arrive at; but there wasn't, there never would be — the exploration alone was more vivid than any finish line. I had been a girl subsumed into a patriarchal music industry, into the 'right' things to listen to, into accepting all-male bands and all-male festival line-ups, men behind the DJ decks and the club night promotions, men in A&R and at the top of record labels. I had stood among those crowds and I had written about those bands and I had fitted myself into the shape of what had been deemed acceptable. Eventually, it had felt too small, too confining. I'd shaken it off, but only now was I really understanding what sound – and listening – could be instead. And now I was finding myself pawing at the boundaries of another category, that of mother, trying to work out what it sounded like.

For years I have moved the clarinet I spent my adolescence playing around the homes I've lived in, always with a slight sense that I may one day play it again. But I've not, and I don't know when or even if I will reacquaint myself with that other universal language, of musical notation. I used to feel shame over this, but I was realising it might have been more complex than that. To pick it up, to try and play, would be to engage with sound in one strict form: that of a specific, perfect note. Of a binary of right or wrong. I recall Senem Pirler's observations about the 'mess' of Pauline Oliveros's Deep Listening practice, how it is about awareness rather than precision. I'd spent so much time trying to find the right way to exist as a woman with a baby that I'd not noticed I'd been living it regardless.

Increasingly, I have been drawn to sounds that are harder to pin down between the five lines of a scale or the inch and a half of a bar. The real or imagined crying of a baby. The light, persistent whistles and hushes that accompany my lived experience of silence. The sounds made in a room full of objects brought together by people who have navigated their whole lives through a kind of listening that has been othered. So much of life exists in the in-between. So much of experience belongs to the finding out rather than certainty. So much delight is born of curiosity. How much more satisfying to encounter and validate atypical experiences rather than cling to patriarchal, neurotypical validity. These sounds surround me; I just haven't been allowing myself to accept I am listening to them. I'd wanted to listen more deeply, and I had thought that involved reconnecting with music, but that feels like a small ambition in comparison to the possibility of encountering a broader spectrum of sound with an open mind and body.

Jané signs off her email with something that shines: 'BSL signs for gold, silver and bronze have this satisfying energy to them that (to me) capture how you might experience them. This resonates with my hopes for E land. To give space to a multi-sensory experience. To more environmental, personal and relational embodied aspects of sound. Understanding sound as an ever-evolving, multi-dimensional reality.'

I bring up YouTube videos of BSL translations for colours, find myself clumsily making the movements with my hands for pink (in the video I am watching, two small swooping taps of the nose with an index finger) and white (middle finger to thumb brought into the chest, and then out as the hand opens). When I see the sign for gold, it is instantly pleasing: hands into fists, brought one on top of another, before releasing open-palmed, like fireworks.

When I compare tutorials I learn, swiftly, that there are variations in the signs for most colours – pink could be a stroke down the cheek, for instance – but for gold every one is the same: a gentle, undeniable, joyful explosion of hands. Silver is similar, only the hands expand after the little fingers touch. I think about Jané's jewellery, the heavy silver earrings that reflected the morning light onto her face. In knowing the signs for these shimmering, precious heavy metals; these rank commodities that have inspired whole socioeconomic shifts; these elusive, glittering heirlooms; I understand them anew. Gold: I bring my hands together, let them float apart. Gold.

By the time I made those small explosions with my hands, by the time I spoke to Jenny about how she listens with her body, sound had been doing strange things to mine for months. Sound had transported me to places I grew fearful of; places that spawned nightmares and warped reality. Certain sounds had left me broken, because they did different things outside the body to inside it. At some point during the days we spent in hospital, something happened to my internal wiring. Perhaps it was in the broom-closet office of the ward sister in A&E, as she frenetically typed and I sat holding a plastic cup of water while my son lay wailing in another room. Maybe it was in the hours that followed, as I swam in uncertainty and sleeplessness and denial, trying to mother an unwell baby, incapable of processing what was actually happening. All I know is that the sound of hearing him in pain, a scream that was once so rare until it became a rampant familiarity, was now hardwired into my being. It was a sound that flooded my body with adrenaline and accelerated my heart rate. It was a sound that made me feel deranged. It was a sound that would take seasons for me to un-hear.

I was not aware of this rewiring happening. I gave myself a week of emptiness to 'recover' from the time we had spent in hospital. The adrenaline would continue to surge through my body for at least a fortnight, then a tidal wave of exhaustion arrived in my bones in its place. Once we returned home the baby was too traumatised to sleep properly and woke several times an hour for several days; his sleep then began to regress. I spent the next few weeks waking up every 45 minutes. I was desperate for rest but, more, I was desperate for normality. I was trying to cope with the new ways sound was reverberating in my life.

ECHOES

Summer was yawning open. The parks filled up with picnic blankets and people. I would lay a sheet out in the garden and sit on the lawn, sweaty in a nursing bra and a pair of shorts, and sink into the ever-elongating hours until I could bathe the baby and put him to bed. These afternoons were quiet: no visitors, nobody else in the house. The air filled with the sound of passing traffic and planes overhead; the occasional insect passing by. Inside my head, it sounded like a jet engine was starting. I was terrified of the baby getting another temperature that could put his life at risk. I couldn't understand how everybody else had moved on, and I remained stuck in this odd, gluey stasis of trauma. I pretended I was fine. I met friends, I went to baby classes. I tried to take my son away for a night with friends in another town but ran back to London before dinner was served; the baby's body felt hot and I didn't have a thermometer. Until I arrived home two hours later, my body vibrated with anxiety.

I decided to travel. The woman I was before I gave birth had made plans to travel. If I travelled, if I took the baby places, I could show everyone how well I was managing. I pleased myself by packing lightly and carrying everything we needed across the city. I wanted to shrug off the small, cosseted newborn world we had been living in. I wanted to fill my brain with new pictures and sounds and feelings, in the hope that they would nudge out the hospital flashbacks that cropped up several times a day. I wanted to be the person I was before all of this happened.

I planned road trips. We drove around the mountains of a tiny Greek island. We drove through the English countryside. We drove hundreds of miles across Italy. If I drove far enough, I thought, I might start to feel normal again. But the baby did not like the car. He did not like sitting backwards or being strapped in. When he was in the car, he cried. I couldn't comfort him, because I was driving. And so, behind the wheel of the car, hurtling down a motorway or navigating a country lane with nowhere to stop, I felt my entire being — my brain, my body, every inch of me that had created the child who was screaming a metre behind me — turn into a kind of emergency. His ratcheting, furious cry was a transportive sound, one that wrenched me back into a hospital ward or the corridor outside it, where I was listening to him screaming in pain. At these moments I was a husk of rage and fear, solely responsible for the safe transit of the two people I love the most in the world.

I expected that the baby would probably have a temperature after his jabs. Other mothers had spoken about it; we had traded tips for Calpol application and naps and how to plan a quiet day afterwards. I couldn't contemplate looking after the baby alone while he grew hot. The little red screen of the digital thermometer had become entirely associated with my son nearly dying. When I took him to the surgery to receive his injections I was a reverberating mass of adrenaline. I hadn't washed my hair in days. When I got there, the doctors told me they did not have my appointment booking, that there had been an error on the system, and the flimsy threads that were keeping me together unravelled. I became the new mother who was not coping. I was a woman crying in a waiting room, demanding that her child get his vaccinations. Eventually, the baby got vaccinated and when he did, he cried in pain. In the end, the noise wasn't as shattering as my weeks-long dread of it; we had all become horribly used to this by now. The doctor, who was kind and concerned, asked how I was doing. I can't remember what I said, but it was enough for him to explain that he would call me the next day so we could 'have a chat'. These three words confirmed what I had been denying: that I was not well.

Stories have long relied on sound to introduce something: a secret, a legacy, a ghost, a truth. The narrator of 'The Tell-Tale Heart' is driven to reveal his crime after being haunted by the imagined rhythm of his victim's heartbeat; Jane Eyre listens out for Bertha Mason's screams and laughter in the night. When Toni Morrison spoke about her writing practice she spoke about music; it offered her, she said in an interview, 'the mirror that gives me the necessary clarity' to tell her stories. She heard her writing; she called it aural literature as a result. Morrison stopped working as an editor in a publishing house to become a novelist full-time; previously, she'd written four novels alongside this job and raising two boys single-handedly. She meditated on the new freedom she was faced with, something that sparked a happiness that caused her to hear her heart, 'stomping away in my chest like a colt'. This was in the Eighties; I have far greater freedoms as a woman than Morrison's generation did, but as she writes in the author's note prefacing *Beloved*, she had more freedoms than those Black women who came before her. There, to the soundtrack of 'the loud heart kicking', she considered the questions of the day – 'to marry or not. To have children or not' – and she thought of enslaved women, for whom 'birthing children was required, but "having" them, being responsible for them – being, in other words, their parent - was as out of the question as freedom'.

Freedom, motherhood and trauma are embodied in *Beloved* through sound. The first character we meet is a baby who is heard but never seen. Her ghost haunts the Civil War-era novel as much as it haunts the house, 124 Bluestone Road, that brings its characters together. She is heard crawling up the stairs. The baby's spirit is so potent it shakes the very walls and floor of the house and tries to kill the family dog. She drives away the community that was once integral to the place: 'there was no one, for they would not visit her while the baby ghost filled the house'. When one character visits, he notes the noise is so loud he can hear it from the road.

The ghost belongs to Beloved, the daughter of Sethe, a character based on Margaret Garner, a woman who escaped slavery only to be arrested for killing one of her children (and the attempted murder of her others) to save them from being returned to the owner's plantation.

When Beloved is an invisible ghost, driving her brothers out of 124 by shattering mirrors and leaving tiny handprints in the cake, she is noisy. Sound, music, song and silence ripple through the text to signify the weight of the many layers of trauma experienced by its characters. There are stories too horrifying for the characters to tell one another; when they were enslaved, they were gagged in ways that have left them speechless decades on. The sounds that Beloved makes as a ghost hold Sethe and Denver in flux: they are haunted by them, but they refuse to escape them, to be once again on the run from something. Denver fashions the hauntings into a sister she only previously knew of as an absence: 'Ever since I was little she was my company.'

When Beloved appears to the family, she has 'new skin, lineless and smooth', a 19-year-old dressed like a lady. But she has a voice that is low, rough and rasping, with a 'song that seemed to lie in it. Just outside the music it lay, with a cadence not like theirs.' It's among the first things that arouse Sethe and Denver's suspicion over this new visitor, along with her uncanny ability to know hidden parts of their lives. It's a voice that stirs Sethe's memories and forces her to re-examine her identity, question her freedom and relive her motherhood.

Autumn arrived. We swapped countries, stopped working for a few weeks, sought out sunshine and afternoon ice creams. Often, the noise inside my head would sound scrambled, like a phone line disconnecting. I developed an inner monologue that made sense to me, but was increasingly challenging to keep company with; it would tell me bitter things that I would accept as truths. It stirred up my deepest fears and ugliest thoughts about myself and muttered them into the many quiet hours I would spend alone with the baby. I was a bad mother. My husband didn't love me. My child didn't like me. My friends didn't enjoy my company. I was loud and smug and annoying. It was my fault, my selfishness, that had allowed my baby to get so ill; I should have taken him to hospital sooner. Sometimes these thoughts formed a kind of constant soundtrack to my day. I would fantasise about ways to escape them; look up flights to other places, plot little getaways, eye up the blades glinting on the magnetic knife rack on the kitchen wall.

All the while, I mothered. I had no option not to. The baby was growing. He was laughing and kicking and rolling, he could clap and would cover himself in yoghurt. I had to keep him safe. I portioned our days into pockets of time when he was awake and when he was asleep. I continued to wake in the night when he stirred, my body alert to his hunger. The noises he made were changing. He very rarely cried in pain any more; even when he was teething he produced a sort of persistent grizzle, rather than a full-bellied wail. He would respond to my singing with his own small utterances, and shape his noises into consonants and vowels.

Four months after the doctor called me up and a referral was made, I was assigned a therapist. The vibrations in my body had calmed down; I was sleeping better, I was able to leave the baby with his father overnight, I no longer flinched when I had to take his temperature. In the first couple of sessions, the therapist asked about my symptoms and I remained fiercely in denial about my state of being. I'd like to work on some other stuff, I told him. We wouldn't need to go over what happened in the summer, what happened in hospital. Slowly, gently, he suggested that we did. The negative inner voice that had been keeping me company wasn't a normal soundtrack that my brain should have been making. The way my body was reacting to the memories of my son crying in pain wasn't healthy. We made a plan for the next three months; we were going to try and deal with my post-traumatic stress disorder.

My conversations with Jané and Jenny had expanded my understanding of what listening could be. Sound was far broader – far more beautiful – than I had allowed myself to realise, and my connection with the noises of the world was something that lay in my body as much as my brain. My matrescence had transformed how I listened, just as sound caused my body to react in ways I was still learning about. Months of suffering with an undiagnosed mental illness had shown me how closely the functioning of my brain was tied to my senses. Sound, and how I listened to it, was informed by what was happening far beyond the machinery of my ears. Breath, movement, interpretation, totality: there was so much else to listen to. The more I tuned in, the more sensitive I could become to what was happening and who was existing around me.

'Sounds affect our bodies so strongly,' composer Annea Lockwood told the *Quietus* in 2021. 'We're not necessarily aware of the entire range of those effects but they're there. Our bodies are responding. That's a connection to the source of the sound. If you can focus on how you feel in response to something in the environment, and then become aware that you feel connected to it, you can move into a state where you don't feel separated from that phenomenon, that strikes me as the actual reality; that we are not in any way separate, much as we have been trained to think of ourselves in that way.' For months I had felt like I was caught between realities, trying to segment myself into categories that never felt completely right in an attempt to understand who I had become. Masking my illness, trying to shrug off the changes I was going through, navigating the different sounds of a baby's cry through a wall. Maybe none of this was separate. Listening might offer me a way of stitching it all together.

I'd first read Annea's name in *Womens Work*, two publications printed in 1975 and 1978 that intended to 'assert that there were many women doing really good work whose names should be more and more familiar', as she'd explained in an interview in 2019. Along with artist Alison Knowles, Annea co-edited scores for performance (text scores, visual scores, musical notation; whatever form the artists wanted to use) by 16 female artists. This was my introduction to her broad and ongoing career, and I asked if she would speak with me about it. Weeks later we connect online, and she speaks about *Womens Work* with pleasing simplicity: 'There would be no discussion, no critique, no overriding essay, just practical. Almost like putting out a recipe book: pieces which you can pick up and do by women artists that we feel are really strong. Do them.' *Womens Work* was accessible, celebratory and inclusive: the artists featured ranged from their twenties to their seventies, they worked across different communities of practice and had different ethnic heritages. Nearly 40 years later the publication was reproduced and a contemporary group of female artists were asked to respond to the original scores. MoMA now exhibits the issues. 'It has an afterlife,' explains Annea, 'which is really what we wanted.'

'You know, I've long thought of listening as a very female activity,' Annea says. 'We're trained to listen to men. We're trained to be attentive listeners. We're trained to be empathic listeners. We're just trained to be good listeners as women. It's part of our socialisation, isn't it?' I say I agree with her, that I've been thinking about this a lot of late. Annea says that while she doesn't think we've achieved gender parity, things are a lot better than when the first issue of *Womens Work* was released. When I ask how feminism intersects with her work she turns the question back on me; she's curious to know what I think rather than wanting to catch me out, but she does nevertheless. As we chew it over I am aware of how much more living and working she has done in much more gendered times than these. 'We're getting there,' she says, diplomatically. 'Maybe it's not so much parity as being enabled to do.'

What has changed since the Sixties, she says, is a broader desire to want to listen. She cites the proliferation of people attending sound walks. 'More and more popular every year, more and more people love doing them, more and more musicians and sound artists offering them and facilitating them. I think it's just an astonishing thing.' Annea has been listening to the environment her entire life; she has learned that to listen is to know and embody, and through that comes a growing awareness of the state of things. 'When people listen to a creek they're aware that it matters, there's a larger context in which to think about it – the health of its banks, whether its polluted or not. We're becoming much more aware of our impact on the environment that other species are having to live with. That's kicking into people's listening.'

Annea's own contribution to *Womens Work* remains her most famous work today: a series of compositions between the late Sixties and the early Eighties that instructed people to follow her in sinking, 'drowning', burying and, best-known of all, burning pianos. We're speaking online; I'm sat at my desk, Annea's sat at hers in what she describes as 'a house on the edge of suburbia, north of New York', but looks like a cabin. It's lined with wood; there are shelves holding books about birds behind her head, and a large picture window out onto trees. She's nearly 85 and the computer camera places her thick, short silver hair centre-screen. Annea smiles a lot, she laughs a lot; she still finds the notion of burning pianos funny. 'The number of times I get asked about what piano burning is all about, it's uncountable,' she says, and there's that laugh again, gleefully distorting her words. Just a few weeks ago she was in The Hague in the Netherlands to give a talk after a screening of a film made when she burned a piano in 1968. There are photographs of it on her website: she's 29 and looks beatnik-y and serious with cat-eye glasses, a hand on her hip a lone white shape against an all-black outfit as the instrument flames behind her. The intention was to make recordings as it burned, but the number of people that gathered around the spectacle meant it was, she tells me, laughing again: 'Totally invalidated. I loved that actually. I loved it at the time. I thought: "This is too funny."'

The long-charred remnants of the piano continue to resonate, she says, because they're 'an easy hook – the playfulness of them, the surreality of them, the sharpness of the idea of burning a piano'. I know this because it's what drew me to Annea's work: this illicit, potent notion of a composer burning an instrument just to listen to the music it makes as it is destroyed.

But what's more intriguing about Annea – and what makes her such a good person to speak to about listening – is that she is still pursuing a project that she began sixty years ago: recording rivers. I find a recording of a 1972 conversation between Annea and Pauline Oliveros online. In it, the 33-year-old Annea, who speaks more softly and with a more clipped accent than the woman who appears on screen before me, speaks about – as Oliveros puts it – 'collecting all the rivers of the world'. Five decades later, we're speaking shortly after she's returned from a field trip to record the Columbia River in Northwest America, something she describes as 'fascinating, and a real challenge'. Annea grew up alongside the Waimakariri River in New Zealand's South Island. She was raised by a man who knew how to cross that roaring stretch of water safely. After studying composition at the Royal College of Music in London, and then furthering her understanding of electronic music in Europe, she was frustrated by the sounds she was making. 'I thought to myself, they don't have any life in them.' Annea turned outwards, to sounds that were 'innately complex, aperiodic and certainly alive', and decided to 'work directly with them. Rivers came into the picture fairly early on.'

A river can sound different, Annea tells me, at dawn and at dusk. It sounds different if it is dammed, like the Columbia is, because it can't flow freely. One of the first rivers she recorded was the Hudson, 'because I was aware that for many New Yorkers it's a visual phenomenon – they have no way of getting close enough to hear it. To hear its energy; it has a very powerful current. I wanted to give people a sense of how strong it is, and how that can come through sound.' She interviewed people who 'felt [the Hudson's] energy directly' and paid particular attention, she says, 'to how sound affects our bodies'. She's still wading in now, getting among the water, extending her listening through her equipment to better capture the multi-faceted parts of a river. 'It's the interior details of the sound which really draw me in, which enable me to feel *with* the phenomenon as opposed to just listening and assessing it. The more detailed the recording, the more alive it is for me. The more alive it is to me, the more I feel like there's a potential to draw listeners inside the sound. I want you to feel that you're right in the river, that you're right inside the sound.'

I wondered how much sound I'd actually been occupying. There were the sounds in my head – the phantom cries, the troubling inner monologue, the noises stuck on repeat that were entwined with my illness – and there were the sounds of the world around me that I was beginning to acknowledge as the soundtrack to my life. But what of inhabiting sound, of getting in among it as Annea did with the rivers of the world? Perhaps sound could exist like a body of water; a moving, alive thing that I could suspend myself in, not unlike the waves and the eddies of the seas and birthing pools and lidos that I'd been so drawn to. Annea, like her contemporary Oliveros, pushed herself into spaces so she could amplify her listening, becoming an extension of the microphone as she enabled its precarious recording of a being more powerful than a human body could ever be. Giving herself over to the noise of it and seeing what happened. My body had been taken over by things that were out of my control – matrescence, trauma, new realms of love and instinct. Perhaps I might learn how to steer through them if I let myself be taken over by sound, too.

Autumn

S OME HABITS DIE HARD. I arrive at the venue minutes before the band come on stage and winnow into the crowd. I'm newly hungry to be among a throng of people, an experience I've not had for months. The journey here has been dislocating; it has been a while since I've travelled across the city at night. But here, in a crowd, between the couples younger than me with their fashionable haircuts and their protective hands and the small groups of friends, I can be invisible out of choice. Among these 5,000 other resonant bodies, I can stand silently with my vulnerabilities.

This is the first gig I've booked a ticket for since I was in my early twenties. The hundreds of shows I've attended since have come with the easy privilege of dropping an email to a publicist somewhere and joining a guest list queue around the side of a venue. I'd booked it on a whim, buoyed by the company of good friends after a long day together, but when it came around I almost didn't go; the set time was later than the bedtime I'd become accustomed to.

Weyes Blood – or Natalie Mering – is performing; the same artist I'd listened to while I was in labour. The artist I'd played on repeat as I walked around Japan on a trip I'd never meant to take alone. The artist who made music I played at my wedding. An artist who, in hindsight, has soundtracked all sorts of transitions in my life, from commutes to childbirth. I've never seen her live: she's always played smaller shows when I've been doing other things. I've never managed to quite motivate my body to get to the other side of London on a cold Tuesday night, or a stage on the other side of a festival. It never occurred to me to buy a ticket and go for pleasure while I was still writing about music for work. But I wasn't that woman any more; no longer a music journalist, simply a fan. A woman in a crowd watching a woman on stage.

Mering appears in a spangled robe and cape that recalls a children's dressing-up box. She's been on tour all year, she says: this is her 110th date. While I was contracting in a birthing pool to her music some seven months earlier, Weyes Blood had been playing the stuff live at the Commodore Ballroom in Vancouver.

The chords strike up and an adoring cry rings out around me – and it rushes out of me, too, as my palms collide. Her band breathes enormity into the rich melodies that swirl out from a Weyes Blood record. 'Her voice is like silk,' a friend of a friend said just before the show, and I can't shake that comparison; I imagine a long ivory drape of it rippling in the air as Mering's glissando floats up and down her lyrics. I've heard her singing hundreds of times before but in seeing it happen live I am struck by the grief of it, the sheer weight of loss and heartbreak and climate anxiety that puddles in her music.

Certain songs are tethers. Tethers to the particular emotional collision of heartbreak and grief and newly-in-loveness that I took to the temples and trails of Japan. It was a period of time that felt life-changing even as I was living it. Then, I was actively travelling to places to heighten my aloneness: tiny villages mostly shut up before the tourist season started, monasteries where I didn't see other tourists, enormous cemeteries blanketed in snow. These were deeply quiet places, ones where silence wasn't sought so much as interrupted – by the chanting of the monks, by the falling of melting snow from a tree branch far above my head, by the jingle of a train pulling into a station. And so, I listened to music as I travelled. A sense of aloneness holds me now, too: I have separated myself from my child and from the friends I arrived at the venue with. I am trying to make the space to listen, perhaps as much to myself as everything around me.

Because I am also travelling through selves, standing here. I have been to this venue several times over my womanhood; I have stood on the stage in the quiet of the daytime and been held rapt, and left part-way through shows because I was bored and arrogant. And I think of these women that I have been as I try to make sense of the one I am now, how separate they all feel.

Mering performs one song, 'God Turn Me Into A Flower', in front of a film that director Adam Curtis has created for it. The huge expanse at the back of the stage holds strange, flashing images: a woman in costume jewellery stoically lifting weights; a woman in a face mask tucking herself into bed and shooing the camera away; an older woman convulsing; a young mother cradling a sleeping child, her eyes shut in a moment of long-fought-for relief. I feel myself connect to the music in similar momentary glimmers. Memories are dredged up and then vanish, like the images on the screen. My breath quickens, my skin prickles, my attention wanders. I am as much part of the crowd as I am outside it. I am embodying something deeply familiar and I am a complete novice all at once.

Almost exactly three years earlier, I'd gone to a gig after another year away from live music. I'd left the newsroom and there'd been a global pandemic; gigs had largely been cancelled across the world. I was wildly self-conscious about going back: I'd not reviewed anything in a while, I'd not really missed gig-going. It was a small, sold-out show by Self Esteem, another female artist whose music had won a close online following during lockdown. She opened with a song called 'I'm Fine', which begins with a throaty, near-imperceptible bassline and ominous drumming, and uses found recording of a woman talking about coping with sexual harassment, in which she explains that she and her friends bark like dogs if they are approached. 'There is nothing that terrifies a man more than a woman that appears completely deranged,' the recording states. When I heard this fill up the arches of the nightclub, women in the audience started to bark. Yips and roars and grunts and growls emerged from the crowd, and I felt a huge smile spread across my face, before I joined in with a lupine howl. It felt like rebellion and community and resilience after a year that had been brutal for women, stuck in their homes and taking on the bulk of the domestic labour and caregiving. We were making a new space of sound, one that hadn't previously existed, one that would vanish in seconds, blurry and amorphous but nevertheless real. In that moment I was inside it, this cacophonous communion of women listening and howling. A space that only we could make, fierce and raw and safe and precious.

In watching Weyes Blood, I realise that I turned up this evening expecting music to imprint itself on me. That I'd bought the ticket as a kind of tacit experiment in establishing just how far removed from music, from going out, I was. But as Mering twirls and sings and lifts her shining sleeves I realise that I'd missed the need — the benefit — of bringing something of myself to this moment: that sound wasn't a passivity but a resonant being, one that I could tune into. If I wanted to engage with sound, if I wanted it in my life, to have it enrich my lived experience and heighten my feelings and deepen my thinking, I needed to participate. I needed to inhabit sound. I needed to be the woman who joined in with strange sisters and howled into thin air.

MIRRORS

That winter I spent a long time craving expanse. I thought about heading north, to Iceland and Scandinavia, curious to know what the emptiness of those unfamiliar landscapes might sound like. I wrote to a friend who lived there and she replied with a list of things she listened to. It included the waterfalls and the silence of the caves, the hiss of steam coming from the ground and the poignancy of the 'constant dripping of the melting ice'. I had come to accept my soundscape – the chug of the dishwasher, my boy's nascent chatter, the voice notes left by my friends – but sometimes it still felt so small.

Every woman I'd spoken to about how they listened had talked about the spaces in which they encountered sound. Annea had waded into rivers. In the noisy quiet of Claire and Jane's lives, misophonia had dictated how they made their homes into sanctuaries from the cacophony of the outside world – both had moved to places of quietude (a village over the bustling city centre for Claire, a tiny flat in a leafy neighbourhood for Jane). Jenny had made a career pioneering new ways of listening and hearing in theatres and performance spaces by developing the aesthetics of access, turning captions and audio descriptions into an integral new part of the art form. For Jané, creating E land – a place of sound and understanding inspired by the confounding wilderness of her childhood – better enabled her to reclaim her deafness.

Place had been crucial to my exploration of sound – the anechoic chamber, the stadium-sized Wall of Sound – but previously I'd separated it from the noises I heard there. Annea's understanding of inhabiting sound suggested they were all connected. It was one thing to embody my listening, but it was another entirely to be equally aware of body, place and sound. And my body and brain had changed so much; a curious shadow version of their previous forms. Pregnancy and birth had pushed and pulled me apart; just as I was physically coming back together, trauma had made everything feel unruly again.

When we come together in listening and reciprocity, we generate things: energy, noise, resistance. We make spaces that hadn't previously existed, that perhaps we had been shut out of or never knew we could inhabit. I wanted to learn how to inhabit sound, to immerse myself within it, but I also needed to understand how to do that as the woman I was now. Some days inhabiting her, listening to her, felt insurmountable. I wanted to push myself into places where sound worked differently. I wanted to stand in new places and let my body, rather than just my ears, listen. I wanted to harness those whispers and breathe life into them. To learn how to occupy this overlooked, undervalued body of sound and make it dance to a rhythm I was still trying to find.

I was increasingly aware of the ambiguity running through all of this, of the soft and osmotic borders between listening and making noise, of inhabiting and embodying. Of the sounds that only some of us hear, of the whispers we tell ourselves and those we trust, of the courage it takes to do or say something without knowing if we'll be believed. My body and my mind had changed and were changing further still, from something hard and fixed and, it transpired, brittle, into something softer, more open and malleable. They felt less known to me but almost stronger for it; of course I was drawn to the shapeless and the uncertain, the spaces we make to feel safe. I spent so many days feeling caught in a changing state of womanhood, I wondered if exploring places of solidity might ground me. If I might find a different resonance in their undeniable heft.

I convince a friend to join me in driving out of the city early on a Sunday morning and head as far as the road will take us, right to the edge of the country. There, we see our destination cresting the horizon from half a mile away: a neat and incongruous rectangle rising above the shrubby trees, dwarfed by the enormity of the cold blue sky above; a concrete curtain across an invisible stage. Here, where land meets the sea, the houses are slung low against the battering salty winds. Stones crunch underfoot.

It's difficult to reach the sound mirrors. I've sent emails months in advance, rearranged visits because they flooded in the relentless rain of the previous seasons. There's no vehicular access: from a small, seaside car park with a broken ticket machine and views of Dover we walk through residential streets until the asphalt peters out. For the next 20 minutes we make our way across scrubby grass and shifting shingle, trying to make out paths of determination underfoot. Once we see the first mirror – the longest, stretching over 60 metres and one of only two this large in the world – we use it as a lodestar. As we get closer, we realise that this mirror, along with two smaller ones, is marooned on an island and accessible only by a swinging bridge. Today the bridge is connected to the other side of the water, something that only happens a few days a year, and after some persuading of a woman with a clipboard, we're allowed to walk across it.

They tower above us, emerging from the stones and the yolk-coloured gorse, both ancient and futuristic at the same time. The sound mirrors are difficult to reach for their own preservation: the bridge was installed in 2003 in a restoration bid; the mirrors had previously been subject to decades of neglect and vandalism. My friend and I are among a handful of equally dedicated day-trippers keen to grab a rare opportunity to experience these sonic dinosaurs up close. There's the couple in their twenties, huddling down near the wind-licked water, microphones in hand; two or three middle-aged men in practical hats with tripods and camera bags and patience. I am the only one without any equipment: I want to see what the mirrors are like with my body alone. I want to hear them, to understand what it is to be in their presence. It feels like a mission that is both wildly simple and borderline impossible.

The sound mirrors – or 'listening ears', as they're known – intrigued me because they represent a rare example of a place created with the sole intent to listen. Microphones pick up noise, hearing aids of varying designs have promised to amplify, but the mirrors were designed to do something else: listen for military threat in an attempt to keep a nation safe. Work began on building the mirrors in the 1920s, with a plan that they would be rolled out across the country to listen for enemy aircraft. As devices they worked – the curved concrete, whether of the long wall or dish-shaped reflectors, which accompany it on the island – reflected the sound of passing aircraft into microphones.

At their best, the mirrors could detect the sound of aircraft 25 miles away, giving the British armed forces 15 minutes to prepare. But what the mirrors couldn't do was keep up with the pace of invention; by the late Thirties the British military was developing radar, and planes were flying too quickly for any detection by the mirrors to be of immediate use. They became an enormous work-in-progress, stopped in its tracks. The mirrors have stood silently listening for the past century.

I'd been preoccupied with what sound might be doing to my body, what it was to listen beyond the use of my ears, to listen with a deeper part of my sense of hearing: with breath and being, to embody the depth of listening that could push my experience of sound into more vivid and strange realms. My body had woken me from the depths of sleep for my son's whimpering and it had conjured a false orchestra in my head that whispered of all the songs and sounds I'd heard before. With each passing day I was navigating sound in new ways, as if I was becoming an instrument that was growing more sensitive, tuning into an ever-greater awareness of sound. But, I was learning, this was only one part of the depth of listening that I craved. Listening well is as much about the external as the internal: I could try and develop perfect pitch, but if I wasn't aware of how my surroundings affected what I was hearing, I'd only be half-hearing.

Up close, the longest mirror looks like a kind of rudimental amphitheatre smoothed out of clay by some giant hand. It's an uncannily calm and clear day; the winds that batter this exposed nub of the country are absent. One of the photographers moans about the lack of cloud cover. I am tuning in. I am listening to the tiniest waves breaking on the water, to the wind that is nudging my hair against my neck, to the low hum of an early bee and the high cheep of birds flying overhead. What was once an RAF base is now part of an RSPB reserve, and this place feels like land that humans can only ever be visitors upon rather than fully inhabit, one made of invisible borders that are nevertheless difficult to cross. It's impossible, really, to imagine the sound mirrors as ever looking new. They wear the signs of age in graffiti and crumbling concrete; slabs pile up behind the longest mirror like broken biscuits. The smaller mirrors, still striking in their scale and their hemispheres, nevertheless carry their own scar tissue and spray paint. Yellow lichen took hold long ago, along with the moss and grass and reed.

We ask the muttering men if we can move in front of their lenses. One of the reasons to visit the mirrors up close, rather than peer at them from the other side of the swinging bridge, is to 'play' on them. The longest mirror acts like a whispering gallery: theoretically, its shape means sound will carry across its uneven surface in spite of volume or weather, as if it were a string between two tin cans. My friend stands at the far end, I stand at the other. She's far away enough to seem smaller than my thumb. Self-consciously, I speak into the concrete: 'Can you hear me?' A pause, and then her voice, undeniably. A whispered echo rising from the grit: 'I can! Can you hear me?' We become childlike at the seeming miracle of it. Her voice is disembodied; it sounds as if it is bouncing along from the middle of the wall. It spooks both of us a bit, this unexpected science.

Standing before the mirrors, my shadow stark against the scrub and the concrete, I think about how long they have been marooned. Even on this day, ripened with sunshine and birdsong, there is an eeriness to them which stems from the fact they were never really used. And yet they've been listening – we just haven't necessarily heard what they've captured. All manner of sounds have reflected across their surfaces, bounced into their weather-beaten microphones. The hum of planes, the call of birds, the yells and whoops and chatter of vandals. Decades have passed along with the planes and the wars and the endless, endless shift of one season into another. Sounds will have been crystallised by ice and baked by heat. Still the mirrors stand, silently.

When I jump down after speaking into the mirror one of the photographers amiably challenges me: 'You didn't believe me, did you? You didn't believe it would work.' I don't know how to answer him. I'd researched the mirrors in the weeks before we came, I knew that they could play this tune. But it was uncanny, the voice I heard echoing back at me — familiar as the one I'd spent hours chatting with in the car but ghostly at the same time. I questioned my hearing, had to check I wasn't hearing what I wanted to, rather than what was there. We said the same thing back and forth, my friend and I: 'Can you hear me? Can you hear me?' We were listening with all of ourselves, our bodies and our minds, and still we begged the question.

And perhaps that makes sense. This island, lonely of people, is a place of contradictions. Silent of the aircraft that inspired the mirrors' creation, but humming with the air traffic of planes that rendered them useless. Devoid of human life but thrumming with animals. We aren't listening to the mirrors, we never really have, but they have listened to us: to the vandals who defaced their surfaces, to the lovers who came looking for solitude, to the devotees who separated them yet further from human life for their own preservation. The noises they conjure are both real and illusory. The mirrors and the water-rimmed land they sit upon occupy something that is almost impossible: the in-between.

I'd come seeking solidity and the hard concrete evidence of forgotten history. When I arrived, I sent a whisper across a wasteland and it was heard anew. This strange place offered me an opportunity to hear in new ways, and in the process, I reciprocated. We made noise, we listened, we connected. We made an invisible new space of sound together across this lichen-studded wall. Through it, I could start to make a way back to parts of myself I thought I'd lost.

WHISPERS

THE SCIENTIFIC COMMUNITY is still trying to prove whether or not the aurora borealis can be heard. After I first learned this, I thought about the Northern Lights for months. I downloaded an app that delivered status updates on global geomagnetic activity; it would offer up a map of the world with varying swirls of auroral activity drawn on it. I could sit on a bus or wait for the kettle to boil and see where there were lights in the sky for the next 30 minutes. When there was a chance of heightened geomagnetic activity in the UK, the app would send a notification. I would sometimes wake in the mornings to learn that there had been an aurora in the small hours in the upper reaches of Scotland. It pleased me when this happened, these little revelations.

I thought about the aurora because I was drawn to the uncertainty of it, these persistent reports of the sound it made even as auroral scientists still struggle to prove that this happens or explain why it might. In embracing the less certain aspects of sound that women encountered, the things we heard that nobody else did, or that nobody else decided to research or write about but which nevertheless existed, here was another whisper: the noise made – or not – by those mesmerising curtains of green and violet that drift across clear, cold skies. I couldn't shake it, the idea that this natural phenomenon could have its own song so slippery and elusive that it defied science. I wanted to hear it, of course, but I was equally intrigued by its ability to persist in the face of scientific reason. Here was a sound that existed in myth and ambiguity that had evaded us for centuries.

Fiona Amery is one of the few academics to research the sounds of the aurora; her 2021 paper, 'The disputed sound of the aurora borealis', is only the fourth work of historical analysis on the topic written in English. She studies corroborating reports of auroral sound from two periods of research that took place half a century apart, the International Polar Year enterprises. These ambitious projects took place across polar countries and research stations in the Arctic and Antarctica in 1882 and 1932. Both sought to find out more about the polar regions' geomagnetism, atmosphere electrics, meteorology, ocean currents and auroral phenomena.

When I call up Fiona at Emmanuel College, Cambridge, she tells me she never intended to research sound; her thesis was on the aurora borealis as a visual phenomenon. But when Fiona was doing her work, sound 'kept cropping up. Whether it was scientists who were very sceptical that there was any sound from the Northern Lights or people local to the northern region saying that they had heard it.' The sources came from several places – Canada, northern Norway, the Shetland Islands – but, Fiona says, 'they were all corroborating each other and talking about the same types of sounds, even though they weren't corresponding with each other because they were talking in their very local forums'. What she saw unfolding 'was a really interesting debate between local people and the scientific community'.

Fiona's sources dated from the 1880s. Nearly 150 years on, she says the notion of auroral sound remains 'very contentious. When I occasionally give talks to modern auroral scientists they're really reluctant to talk about the sounds because it's just considered this weird quackery, or wishy-washy science that they're really not interested in. But then among Indigenous communities, who have oral traditions, they fully accept that the sounds exist: it's part of their tradition, part of their everyday lives. It's interesting: who you talk to changes the language quite a bit, depending on whether you're talking about something that is considered real and exists, or whether you're talking about something that is only a potential.' Here it was, a whisper: something heard, something knowable. Something difficult to define or pin down but still there enough to be sought out.

Both the first and the second International Polar Year projects championed then-cutting-edge forms of technology: new-fangled gadgets that tried to capture and measure the aurora. What's notable, Amery argues in her paper, is that the expedition members continued to trust and rely upon corporal accounts of the aurora: bodily and sensory experiences informed the IPY's findings in spite of the scientific machines they had access to. 'It went against the grain of a lot of twentieth-century atmospheric physics,' Fiona explains. 'Generally, senses are almost exclusively replaced with instruments. So the fact that actually people's bodies were being used to register the sound — that I found interesting.'

The researchers tried listening to the aurora themselves — as Fiona writes, they 'would sit alone in silence for hours on end . . . watching, listening, and waiting for the aurora' — but they also undertook surveys. In 1885 several thousand letters were sent across Norway asking for anecdotal reports of auroral sound; 114 responses came back, of which 92 showed belief in the sounds, 53 claiming to have heard the noises themselves and 39 quoting someone else's experience. These anecdotal reports emerge from unconnected corners of the Arctic Circle and at different times: there's no way, Fiona points out, that the people making them could have otherwise traded notes. 'There are so many accounts, it seems like it must have a sound,' she tells me. The author of one paper compared the sounds of the aurora to 'the quiet but rapid rubbing together of two pieces of paper' and wrote that he heard these noises in northwest Copenhagen three times in five years. The survey responses could be equally evocative. Some described the aurora as sounding like 'burning dried juniper', 'tearing silk' and 'the buzzing of a bee': all means, Fiona writes, of capturing 'some mode of whizzing, crackling or hissing, often quiet sounds on the edge of perception'.

I am struck by the beauty of these analogies and how multi-sensory they are. To read them is to imagine the smell and the spit and the heat of branches on a fire, of the physical wrench and frayed fibres of ripped fabric (in my mind, the silk was the colour of dirty snow, caught between two firm fists), and the warmth and stillness of an early summer's morning among the flowerbeds. I'm drawn to that qualifier in Fiona's paper – that these sounds, these active, embodied, unusual sounds, are 'often quiet [and] on the edge of perception'. They are barely there, but they are nevertheless undeniable. They are sounds that are ambiguous but persistent, reaching out for connection – and surviving, in spite of the scientific institutions that want to deny them, in spite of the fact they are almost impossible to either prove or disprove. What Fiona set out to show in her paper wasn't so much whether the aurora made sound or not, but that the men researching the Northern Lights trusted their bodies over their instruments. But when I ask her opinion on the sounds, she says she believes in them – there are simply too many corroborative accounts for something that couldn't be heard.

When it comes to whispers, corroboration can be potent – for better and worse. Arguably, this is the landscape in which conspiracy theories bubble up, where people conflate disparate pieces of information into what they want to believe and present opinion as fact. We live in a time when we are served up information that algorithms and artificial intelligence believe we might be interested in, not with the intention to broaden our minds or spark our curiosity so much as to confirm suspicions and breed half-truths. We live in a time when self-selecting online communities can have enough sway to challenge democracy: we've never been more sceptical or questioning of what we encounter, and we've never needed to be more cautious about what we're presented with. Over the seasons that I'd become preoccupied with the aurora, that I'd found an unlikely reassurance from the notifications about it on my phone, I'd been listening to whispers of my own making: ones that were a hangover from the summer I'd lived through, an inner voice that cast fable and confusion I struggled to make sense of.

It had made me even more determined to examine the

sonic ambiguities I was encountering. The fact that we don't know if the aurora makes sound or not is almost more attractive than if we knew for definite that it did. It begs a question that we turn to answer with our bodies, as those who heard it in Fiona's research did, to try and understand. Fiona knows this feeling first-hand – of relying on a body to listen, rather than an instrument. A couple of years ago she was taken to Svalbard by a documentary film crew who wanted to try and hear the aurora. She admits she was sceptical – 'I was aware that the sounds are very rare. Even if you live in a place where you see lots of Northern Lights, even then, people live their whole lifetime and only hear them once. I was only going to Svalbard for three days; I didn't know if we were going to see the Northern Lights at all' – but something unexpected happened.

Fiona didn't hear the lights, but she did listen for them: a process that was surprisingly affecting. 'I got a lot from the rehearsing or replaying some of the emotions of listening, of being in some of those spaces and seeing the Northern Lights and then straining your ears to hear if there was anything going on.' On one of the nights during their trip, the team Fiona was with were treated to a 'very strong and very active' auroral display – something that defied the forecasts. They quickly gathered their things and moved to an area that was as flat as possible. 'We were just sitting and gazing up at the sky, very conscious not to be moving too much so that we didn't make any sounds ourselves,' she tells me. 'I suppose there was a lot of anticipation, a kind of tension in the air. That we hoped for the sound, that we almost were feeling for it, putting out tendrils to bring in the sound. But also, because the Northern Lights were so active themselves, it was sort of possible to imagine what the sounds might be like.'

For the previous four years, Fiona had sat with the voices of researchers and Indigenous people, of local people and survey participants, all of whom were born decades, if not more than a century, before she was. Sitting in the very cold, very dark wilderness, she was able to embody their written experiences in a new way. 'I think it was my way of connecting with a lot of my historical actors, because I was imagining that a lot of people that I've been reading about have watched the Northern Lights just as I have. They felt similar wonder and amazement and they've also sat quietly, staring at it, wondering what it's going to do, not really expecting it to be there. They felt a lot of those things so I felt very connected, even to the very gestures and emotions that they might have felt,' she explains. 'That gave me a lot of insight into their thoughts really, as well as their hopes and interest and fascinations.' It's an activity she called 'rehearsing or replaying the emotions of listening'.

The Northern Lights didn't make any sound that night — not that Fiona could hear, at least — but that didn't stop her from listening in a new way. There, on the snow-covered, frozen expanse of Svalbard, she was able to tune into the whispers she had been tracing in documents and archives. In undertaking a very hopeful, very active performance of listening, she was able to do so through time. The papers she'd researched came closer to the imaginary ones rubbing together, and making sound, in the sky a century before.

Word spread through the internet. It was almost bedtime and Matt walked out the back door; there were posts online saying that the sky was filled with colours. The AuroraWatch app – still installed on my phone months after I'd downloaded it – had been sending out more notifications than usual. If I opened it the whole phone screen filled with red; the chart that usually burbled away quietly showing no chance of sighting the Northern Lights in the UK was at a fever pitch. The forecasts, at least, suggested the aurora would be visible by human eye across the country – even in our southern city.

It was the end of a long day; the baby and I had been outside for nearly all of it, both of us grubby with wet soil and berry juice. I was tired and sceptical as I pushed myself into the garden and looked up. I searched the tight, built-up rectangle above our garden, not entirely sure what I was expecting to see. The sun hadn't long set, there was still a distant glow to the west. To the immediate east, the pale orange burn of the streetlamp I so often longed to switch off. Windows in the flats opposite without their curtains drawn. Directly above was a substance that looked like egg white in water; an entangled being I initially dismissed as a cloud. But it was the only one in an otherwise clear sky: the moon was so well-cast that you could see the faintest pale rim around its dark side. I raised my phone camera up towards the shape and saw stars pierce through it, saw colours appear on the screen – drifts of turquoise and an echo of cerise.

I played a game with myself, one of belief and understanding. Could this be the aurora, here, against these never-dark skies? Perhaps it was, perhaps this was our share of extraordinary colours, of dancing electromagnetism. I stood in the garden and listened. I heard the crescendo of a speeding motorbike engine tear through the roads beyond, the background white noise of Brixton, grinding and crunching and throbbing away. No human noise, no music. By some standards it was quiet. I thought about the noises Fiona Amery had encountered in her research, that of tearing silk, the buzzing of a bee or of dried juniper burning. These noises weren't here either. The crackling or hissing, 'often quiet sounds on the edge of perception', could have been applied to the background noise of my urban back garden, to the soft chorus of tyres trundling beyond the wall. In the decades that have passed since those accounts were made, the world has grown loud.

I had been searching for whispers and diving into ambiguities, drawn to the not-quite-there sounds, the messy presence required of an imperfect Deep Listening practice. Faced with noise, then with silence, I'd searched for the in-between, something to listen to that reflected my own uncertain state. When I'd stood in the Integratron and asked what sound could do, I heard my voice surround me in polyphonic shades, as if they were different selves I was trying to piece together. I'd whispered then, like I had against the enormity of the sound mirrors, and since then there had been more whispers besides: rumour and promise, held by the skies above us.

I thought of Fiona's memories of watching and listening to the aurora on Svalbard with her documentary team. Of how she went out into the snow and lay very still, how she hushed her breathing to increase her chances of hearing and, in the process, placed herself in the bodies of those people whose accounts of the aurora had led her there. Just as she had rehearsed the emotions and gestures of listening, so I was too, standing outside my back door on a Friday night, questioning the skies above me. It was impossible, in that moment, for me to understand this as a solitary experience. While I was alone – Matt was inside, I saw no neighbours, heard no other voices of people watching – I wondered who else was putting their bodies through the same actions. I thought of all the people who had also taken their bodies from the comfort of their homes and craned their necks and opened their senses, all the while living and breathing that questioning state of hope without even knowing what it was they might be looking for. I felt a communion with them, these other unknown hopefuls, looking to the skies just as thousands of people have done before, for thousands of years, exhaling in wonder.

February

Monday lunchtime and I'm sat at my desk. It's been like this every week recently: the baby naps and I sit here and join a virtual meeting where I am coaxed through those days in hospital by a therapist. It's a strangely intimate thing to do with someone I've never properly met, but he is kind and supportive and I am increasingly aware that I have been poorly papering over the cracks of what happened to me the summer before, so I sit there while the baby sleeps and do as he says.

The sessions follow a formula. The memories in my brain are disordered, he explains. Bit by bit, we will try to tidy them up. Each session is dedicated to a different part of the process: reliving the trauma, updating my memories of it and then reclaiming it. The sessions are recorded and arrive in my inbox hours after we have finished; my 'homework' is to watch them back. It is such a trivial little word for it. Home. Work. So much of my work is at home, these days. So much of my home is work. I play the recordings at the kitchen table while I eat dinner. I play them as I wash up. At these times I am splintered across several places at once: at the sink, removing cooking oil from a pan; at my desk on a Monday lunchtime; in a hospital corridor on a beautiful summer's evening, waiting for my son to get the drugs he needs.

When we make these recordings, I am sheltered a little from my own voice. The therapist encourages me to close my eyes and I wear large headphones that muffle the rest of the world. I talk him through what happened months before and, minute by minute, he nudges me through the moments that my brain will replay afterwards, when I'm walking to the shop or sitting in a children's centre. What does that feel like, he asks? Any eloquence I may possess evaporates: 'It feels shit. It feels really shit.' What are we saying on the scale of intensity, here? 'Eight.' That's a biggie, he says. Stay with it.

We stay with it. We stay with returning to hospital just as we thought we would spend the night at home. We stay with my memories of standing in a corridor trying to find the right distance from the sound of my son screaming in pain. We stay with shouting at a nurse after a long day and many sleepless nights, because it feels like we have been abandoned and I am convinced that, if he does not receive the correct drugs in the vanishingly small window we are now left with, he will die. We stay with it. And then I replay it, over and over again, because I am told that this is the best way to get better. As I replay it, I become familiar with the patterns and pauses my voice makes when it tells a story; the feeble, misguided attempts to inject some levity into this thing. The half-laughs, the barely perceptible scrunch of a tissue against a cheek. I listen to another version of myself; I listen to the sounds of a body I have been occupying but barely recognise. Postpartum, scrawny with stress. She looks old, she looks a bit beaten down by it all.

In the weeks that follow, the therapist and I revisit the recordings and we revisit, in our minds, the hospital wards and the blocky purple wipe-down couches and the *Lion King* posters on the walls of the treatment rooms. When we revisit these memories, we 'update' them. I'm told to embody another kind of self; one who can look back at the woman losing her mind at a nurse or pacing a vinyl floor and offer her some empathy. Often, this happens in the form of conversations that are impossible – they span time and space. They are imaginary. They exist only in my mind; it's why they are powerful.

And that is how I end up being several versions of myself all at once. The woman in the hospital corridor, cowering from the sound of her son being cannulated; the woman telling the story seven months later; the woman listening back to it; and this new, still-weary version of myself, telling her that the noise he is making is tearing her apart because it is meant to, that she is his mother, and of course she can't be there: she needs to remain as intact as possible so she can care for him afterwards. This Russian doll set of fractured bodies, telling stories through space and time and internet cables.

After months of letting my own mangled thoughts narrate my life, I finally receive some deliverance: I didn't let him down, I didn't fail; I reacted in the only way that would allow me to hold him and keep holding him. The negative inner voice that has been so tormenting and so believable is straightened out, like a bedsheet. Finally, among all the noise, a feather-light whisper of rationality.

PHONE LINES

When I first started thinking about listening, I thought about the people whose listening others rely upon. I thought about how we raise girls to be 'good listeners' and how much listening, as both an active and passive state, sits upon the shoulders of women who are already undertaking so much mental labour. Before I understood sound to be anything more than a binary existence of noise and silence, before I'd learned about all the different ways that women listened – with their bodies and with brains that processed sensory information differently – I thought about the more technical side of listening. Of the people who listen as a job or a vocation; the people who listen underwater to track the locations of whales, for instance, or in the call centres of the emergency services, whose daily decisions transform the lives of others.

I thought about all the things that can happen down a

phone line. One of the key memories of my childhood is of my mother – who stopped working for the best part of 16 years to raise us – tucked in a corner of the hallway of our home. There, with her back against the wall and her legs against the floor, she would sit and talk to people – friends, her family, the various strangers at banks and schools and insurance companies who needed dealing with – the cream telephone cable a kind of barrier between our sticky, *Sesame Street*-inflected world and the adult one she occupied. At times it felt like she spent so long on the phone, but I imagine most calls only lasted a few minutes. Since giving birth, I have spent more time sending messages on WhatsApp than I could have ever thought possible: to friends, to other mothers, to my family. I suspect my son will grow up with memories of me leaving voice notes and tapping things out, one-handedly, as I cook his tea or push his buggy along the pavement. The phone calls I make are short and practical, but the phone is still a lifeline to another, adult realm beyond the confines of the domestic one that has arrived with our child. It allows me to escape the sometimes grinding, sometimes saccharine existence of baby land, where my tone sits high and bouncy, an unanswered rhetoric of naps and milk and snacks. Through my phone I can hear the voices of my friends and the flotsam of the life they are living at that moment – sirens, or birdsong, or the tap running. The technology has changed, but the tether is the same. On some days it feels life-saving, that connection to a world of adult noise.

For weeks the therapist had been listening to me, delivered through the council's mental health service onto my computer screen. Sometimes I dreaded these sessions, sometimes they felt like a chore. At other times, though, they were a much-needed release. For an hour, sometimes 90 minutes, I was able to unfurl to someone whose job was to listen to what I had to say. It often felt like a kind of lottery win, to be occupying someone else's time in this way.

For years, my work had involved listening to people in an attempt to get them to tell their stories. I had developed my own ways of trying to make space for them, to tune into what people were saying and make sure I held that as best I could. But this was different. I was being listened to as a means of medical intervention. The therapist was listening to me, making space for what I was saying and helping me to make sense of it so I could change how my inner monologue sounded. Being listened to by a stranger was changing the constant soundtrack of my thoughts.

It's grown dark by the time I call her. I pass the baby to my husband with instructions about his dinner, head out of the house to the shed in the garden and switch on the desk lamp. It's a Friday evening and Brixton is gearing up for the weekend; people getting ready and bars opening, sound systems vibrating in rooms and cars in the tussle of streets. And here, alone, I'm suspended between these two peripheries of light – one from the kitchen, a few metres away, and one from the lamp – as I tap the 11 digits into my phone and wait for Paulina to pick up.

She's in Cambridge, in the same house she's lived in for decades. In the same room, by the same desk, where she would take calls on Friday evenings from women she didn't know. Paulina Palmer is in her eighties now and a semi-retired academic. But in the late 1970s she was part of a movement of feminists who created spaces of listening for women forced into solitude and secrecy because of their sexuality. In 1979, with her lover at the time, and a handful of friends she'd made through a feminist self-defence group, Paulina set up the Cambridge Lesbian Line from a secondary phone line she installed in her spare room. It was open to callers on Friday evenings. 'It's quite interesting,' she says with a wry laugh, 'making this call in the very same room.' Paulina's voice is clipped but warm; the phone line slightly frazzles the edges of her words.

The Cambridge Lesbian Line emerged when, as Paulina puts it, being gay was 'a really difficult business'. Homosexuality between men had only been legal since 1967. Section 28, Margaret Thatcher's oppressive legislation that banned the 'promotion of homosexuality' (in real terms, educating about or even discussing homosexuality, particularly in schools), was passed in 1988. At first, it might seem like the two decades in between were a halcyon time of acceptance, but the reality was far from it, Paulina tells me: 'In those days, lesbian and gay people were ostracised; if they taught in schools, for instance, they often lost their jobs [if they became known as gay].'

Phone lines like Paulina's offered closeted and curious people the opportunity to discuss something that was still taboo in British society. In the Seventies, even the word 'lesbian' wasn't openly used beyond lesbian social circles, as Helen Bishop, one of the women who set up the first Lesbian Line – in London, in 1977 – wrote in *Trouble & Strife* magazine in 1992. 'The new Sexual Offences Act in 1967 had made gay men's lives easier, but lesbians were still not really on the map and suffered from the fact that the only thing the general public really knew about us were the stereotypes presented in films like *The Killing of Sister George,*' she continued (the 1968 film shows an ageing lesbian actress assaulting two young nuns in the back of a cab). Representation of lesbians in society was so scant that the London Lesbian Line became the go-to authority on lesbianism in the country; when women from the Line accepted speaking requests from groups ranging from universities and counsellors to the National Housewives' Register (a social group for women), they were frequently met with surprise. 'You could see their mental processes written all over their faces,' co-founder Shauna Brown is quoted as saying in the magazine. 'They had expected some sort of freaks, sort of monsters, and there we were, perfectly ordinary women of all ages, to whom they could relate.'

While the women behind the London Lesbian Line were fielding more than 200 calls a week, Paulina and her then-partner Linda were getting the Cambridge Lesbian Line on the wires. Society is hardly free from homophobia now, but it's nevertheless difficult to imagine quite how risky setting up an explicitly lesbian phone line was nearly 50 years ago. Four women, including Paulina, thrashed through the practicalities of the line before encountering the problem of advertising it: without word of it being published, closeted women who needed the line wouldn't know it existed. 'Two people volunteered to go along to the *Cambridge Evening News* and talk to the editor about it,' she explains. 'Quite bravely, I think, because of course in talking to him it was revealing that they were gay. He didn't want to take any advertisement for us at all, he said he wouldn't. But we contacted them again; by then he'd talked to the head of the newspaper, and they decided it was all right. That really was the way we got going.'

Paulina's house had been chosen to host the line for practical reasons – she was older than the other founders and she had more room than them. But she still speaks of the wariness hosting the line instilled in her; the need for anonymity was very real. 'We didn't want it to get out to anybody; we didn't want it to even get out to the feminist group here really, unless they identified as lesbian.' (It was only in the early Seventies that the Women's Liberation Movement began to recognise and align with lesbianism.) 'We really did want to keep secret because of my house: people could come. I was really scared about this, people could come and throw stones through the window.'

The dedicated Cambridge Lesbian Line was established and its co-founders began to rota shifts on Friday evenings. But the line was quiet. 'It was terribly disappointing at first, we got no calls at all. Even though there was this advert, nobody rang.' Nobody rang for six months. Then, just as the group were considering giving up, the women started to call.

'I think we thought that women of our age, who lived in Cambridge, would be the ones to ring us, but that didn't happen so much,' Paulina tells me. 'We tended to get calls from outside Cambridge, from the provinces; most of the women who rang were older than us, and several of them were married and had a lesbian past; they'd lived somewhere else, perhaps London or a city, and then decided to get married because being gay could be isolating in that period unless you'd found a group of people. Now, they were married, and they didn't find marriage as what they'd thought. They rang us up to discuss their experience and ask what they should do. It was difficult.'

The London Lesbian Line had been the first dedicated lesbian phone line in the country, and began as a nation-wide offering; later, when lines such as the Cambridge one (among the earliest regional lines to be set up) appeared, the London line directed callers to their local lines. It had been partially set up by women who had worked on Gay Switchboard and Icebreakers, phone services set up primarily with men in mind. These women were in the minority – four women among the 25-strong collective of Icebreakers, while Gay Switchboard had 5 women and 75 men on the lines. When women did call, they would frequently speak with gay men.

The London Lesbian Line immediately had callers. Nearly 20 years later, co-founder Rachel Beck told *Trouble & Strife* that she'd later met the first caller – Rachel must have told the woman calling her name, and that she was the first to get through. 'She said it had changed her life.' Recalling the Line's creation and impact at a Lesbian History Group meeting in 2021, Helen Bishop said: 'I used to go home after doing a night on the phones with a real feeling of "I've done something". A real feeling that, no matter how hard it was, or how frustrating, that we had given something and that was the most rewarding thing about the line for me.'

'The idea was that you could change someone's life in 20 minutes,' co-founder Pam Isherwood added. 'Lesbian Line was the only thing, in that bit of time, a very, very direct contact with one woman, turning her life around. Just by saying to her: "It's perfectly all right to be lesbian. You are completely normal. You can be happy. There will be a future for you."'

The calls, the founders suggested in their recollections, often came from frightened, ashamed and confused women. From the beginning, the line operators in London took notes of every call, and these were then coded into 'about ten types of call', ranging from the simple – about the timings and locations of certain lesbian club nights – to the serious, including domestic violence. Both Paulina and the London Line founders were familiar with custody battles, as the judicial services at that time could refuse a woman access to her children if she had left her husband because she was gay. 'It was very hard, those were some of the calls where I came off the phone in tears, just from feeling what they felt like,' Helen remembered, 'especially if they had kids, because they didn't have the walkout option. Lots and lots of women lost their kids.' The line tended to take a different approach to others' on matters of homosexuality within the home; specifically, in the necessity of safeguarding their lesbianism. 'With married women, the first thing we would say is "Don't talk to anyone. Do not tell your husband, even though he's ever so nice and you love him and you've been with him for thirty-seven years – don't tell him yet,"' Pam said. Line operator Lynne Keys remembered the shock among the group when they learned the Samaritans had advised lesbian women to speak with their husbands about their predicament: 'So many of us knew: as soon as he felt that you no longer desired him, he was going to punch you, throw you on the street, get custody of the children.' Some married women didn't want to leave their husband so much as they needed an outlet to share their secret heartbreak when an affair with a woman ended, Helen said: 'They were on the phone in tears because they couldn't express their upset anywhere. They had to have a mask on, with their husband, their family. That was very hard. We would say it was okay what they did, that they didn't have to feel bad about it, that we knew they had to parcel it up.'

Sometimes the calls weren't about lesbianism at all: Lynne recalled a conversation in the early Nineties from a closeted member of the army who had been part of the Iraq invasion during the Gulf War and needed to talk about the atrocities she had witnessed there. 'She wanted to talk, and it came out slowly,' Keys said during the History Group meeting. 'I remember being on the phone for ages, listening, talking, asking questions. We talked for a long time. And she said, "I don't know what else I can say, really, but it was so good talking to you because I have no one else to share this with, these terrible things." I thought it was horrendous; these lesbians are going through so much and the only place they can ring is

Lesbian Line.' I wonder how long the caller had waited until she'd picked up the phone, dialled the number and waited for her call to be answered. I wonder how she came across the number, how she made the decision that it could be an outlet for her – a much-needed space of listening, where she could say all the things she'd been keeping down. I suspect the woman calling was loved by people, but sometimes it's easier to know the person listening is a stranger. I thought of the GP calling me up after I'd burst into tears in his office. I thought of all the things I had said to the therapist. There's a privacy and an intimacy in listening down a phone, or with someone you'd not recognise on the street, that makes it more powerful.

'You had to listen, and listen absolutely,' Helen said, about taking the calls. Pam earned a reputation for her skill at handling the silent calls, which made up 20 per cent of the total received: women sitting at the other end of the line, terrified to say anything. Each silent caller would be granted ten minutes, Pam said – 'after that, you know you're not going to get anywhere' – before they would be told another call had to be taken, invited to call back another time and asked to hang up: one of the line's rules was that a genuine call would never be hung up on. Pam would run through the line's purpose and offerings, and then invite them to tap on the phone to show they were still on the line. Sometimes she'd encourage a giggle by asking them what their favourite ice cream was, for instance. At other times, women would call back ready to speak, admitting that they had called three times before but hadn't been able to talk. These instances proved Pam's theory right, that keeping talking was crucial because at the other end of the line there was 'just a desperate, desperate, desperate bloody woman, hanging on for her life, and you have to keep her there'.

What swiftly became apparent – and perhaps of greater surprise to Paulina and the team in Cambridge – was that some of the women were ringing the line as a first step towards meeting other women in person. 'The main thing was: was there any way of meeting up with lesbians?' Paulina tells me. 'We'd never thought of that. We thought women would ring the line for help or something, or talk about an experience, we didn't think they'd be wanting to meet other people. We thought they probably would know some; but these women didn't, who lived in the provinces.'

Speaking with Paulina, the overriding sense I get of what the Cambridge Lesbian Line offered is that it was a means of breaking through the isolation that some of their callers – the elderly women living alone in villages, the ones caught between a secret relationship with a neighbour and a loveless marriage – experienced. Quite simply, she says, 'they had nobody to talk to'. Paulina, who lost her father when she was nine and credits her mother for the innate feminism and support she was raised with, said creating the Line was integral to her gender politics; this was a space of listening imbued with radical politics. 'I didn't find the listening a problem. I think some of the people who wanted to work on the Line actually found it a bit difficult, and we did talk about that when they joined the Line. We knew that one of the most important things wasn't so much the talking but just listening; often the women who rang had been extremely isolated and had nobody to talk to, and just letting them talk was crucial.'

Actually meeting the women who called was rare, though. By the middle of 1978, the London Lesbian Line was fielding 500 calls a month. 'What happened to their lives?' Helen posited during the History Group meeting. 'We don't know, because they were anonymous. We only had a name, and it wasn't necessarily their real name, but we only had a name to identify them in the logbook.' Meet-ups would consist of half a dozen women, on average. 'We're talking about tens of thousands of phone calls,' Pam pointed out. The *Trouble & Strife* article was published to mark the Line's 15th birthday, in 1992; there's a polite plea at the end: 'Have you ever phoned the Line? Write and tell us what it meant. You can write anonymously if you prefer, and nothing will be used without the writer's permission. It would be interesting to have the perspective from "the other side" on Lesbian Line's first fifteen years.'

It would run for a further sixteen, closing in 2008 after years of tricky financial wrangling. Paulina hung up her dedicated phone for the last time in 2002. She tells me the calls were dying down – there were more openly lesbian events and magazines available; gay women weren't as desperately isolated as they had been 25 years earlier. I think about what these women created in terms of aural space. The thousands of calls, the hours of listening, the precious anonymity to be found at the end of wire, the unquantifiable comfort offered by the click of a line. How the collectives managed to create connection through thin air, and the women calling found courage in the tapping of a finger on the hard plastic of a receiver. The lines were born of a desire to be seen and help others come to terms with their identity. The value in what these women created for others can't be denied: an accessible space (as the London Lesbian Line became established, measures were put in place for d/Deaf people and those with accessibility needs) that was often the last refuge for many women. A space in which they could be listened to without judgement.

While this space had an almost liminal existence, at times – of voices travelling electronically along wires – the phone lines emerged from embodied feminist action and created points of connection that pushed the existence, identity and rights of gay women into the mainstream. The London Lesbian Line took part in political marches, supported Labour MP Maureen Colquhoun, who was deselected on account of her sexuality and appeared on national television, bringing the word 'lesbian' – still an oddity at the time – into homes across the country, in many cases for the very first time. This was a lifeline that existed both invisibly – through the surreptitious phone calls made by desperate women on shared phones, or ones paid for by their husbands – and also in vivid colour, broadcasting a whole previously hidden part of society.

It is bittersweet that the success of these phone lines also spelled their disappearance. There are other factors at play too, namely the sociopolitical structures that enabled their creation and funding in the past five decades which no longer exist. But, as the demise of the Cambridge Line demonstrates, women stopped calling the lines because they no longer felt quite so alone. From giving women the confidence and permission to come out to themselves – something Pam pointed out 'is possibly not much easier now than it ever was' – to helping them meet other lesbians and opening up societal acceptance of gay women, these phone lines made lesbianism less of a secret. With each phone call, the collective created more of an acceptance that made the line increasingly redundant.

And so, the lines themselves risk becoming a footnote of LGBTQI+ history: Paulina is in her eighties now, the founding members of the London Lesbian Line among the oldest in their community. The lines are disconnected. The women who once called are living all manner of unknown lives. Even the call logs, meticulously kept and, in the words of Pam, 'the most precious documents', are inaccessible to the public due to data protection laws. This space of listening now sits quietly — whether in an archive in Glasgow Women's Library or in the memories of those who created it, in recordings and old magazines.

In the Lesbian History Group recording, you can hear Helen and Pam and Lynne close their panel discussion with a question: should the Line exist again today? Is there a need for it? The group are resounding in their approval. There are other means of connection now: even beyond the events and the festivals there is the enormity of the internet. When you can find other women to meet through a dating app, what can a phone line offer? The group talk about young women, of the value in having someone to speak with. Then Pam makes an argument that I can't shake: 'But who can you ring up when you're heartbroken?'

TRANSLATION

I WAS PREOCCUPIED WITH THE notion of belief. Externally, my life had moved on. But in between the new moments of clarity my head was still a mess of noise. Starting treatment – being listened to – was helping, but it also caused a number of things that I had clumsily managed to quieten to crescendo. When I collected my son up from childcare the old misleading narratives that had emerged in the wake of his illness – that he didn't like me, that he smiled for the nursery staff more, that they thought I was an unfit mother, that they knew better – beetled into my ear. The reverberations of trauma echoed through my body during the now-quiet days I had sometimes longed for; I would be restless and twitchy at my desk, not knowing what I needed to calm down. When I took a break, I'd check the baby's room, convinced he was having a nap when he was actually in a different building entirely, a 10-minute walk down the road. Much of what I sat with was a sense that what I had experienced wasn't enough to justify this level of brokenness. My husband was functioning fine. My son was happy and well. Nobody seemed to want to discuss what had happened – they hadn't for months. I had conjured this relentless racket inside my head over nothing at all; it was the work of a fantasist, a weakling. Often, I felt caught adrift on an island of my own making, tormented by ill winds that were headed only my way. I would find myself in competition with these narratives, desperate for a calm, logical voice to tune into. I'd been drawn to the sounds of the uncertain and the ambiguous because they reflected my own formative state, but I wondered what it would be like to be certain of sounds. To be so sure of what you are hearing that you will stand by it, insist upon it, at all costs.

When we overhear something, how does that listening differ? There is listening to create, listening to forge understanding, to deepen our bodily experience, and there is listening for danger – or, on that other side of the same sharp blade – safety. The people who sit at the phones trying to connect with closeted women, or abused women, or women who have just taken an overdose; they listen with an intent fuelled with urgency. I so often felt like I was translating: my memories, the warped flashbacks caused by trauma, the meaning of my son's crying in the night, my own glitchy inner voice. What of the women who listen to total strangers in other countries, who may be forging plots that wouldn't just put a person's life at risk but several; what do they hear? What if your job was not just to listen, but to translate; to be the ears of understanding and connection between irrelevancy and risk? What if the way you heard a hesitancy or an intake of breath made the difference between life and death, not just for one person, but for a nation at large? That level of certainty felt so far away for me.

The Doughnut, as the headquarters of the UK's intelligence, security and cyber agency is affectionately known, is a short walk from a suburban roundabout. It's the nucleus of the Government Communications Headquarters – or GCHQ – and it's almost too big to take in. There are the gates and the fences topped with shining coils of spined wire, and enormous satellite dishes, which rise above, constantly listening. Then another building, where a trio of genial older men in shirts and ties gently rid me of anything electronic, before checking my ID. I am left waiting in the reception of this grand antechamber, the security before the security, trying to hold on to the various instructions I have been given to get through the gates ahead, with the alien notion that I will be met by my contact in the near future, despite having no way to get hold of them. Without my various devices – laptop, phone, Dictaphone, headphones, Kindle – I feel listless and unmoored. I clutch my notebook and pen, like a child on a school trip.

I'm here to meet with Tia and Jill, two linguists who have worked for GCHQ for 17 years. Jill, who wears a studious air and a Scottish burr, joined a couple of months after Tia, who seems too young to have worked here so long, and smiles a lot. They came to GCHQ as linguists after, among other things, studying languages in childhood. Here they have learned to listen in ways that many of us wouldn't have even thought possible. They listen in to recordings of people having conversations over long periods of time; they become familiar with these strangers, with their vocabularies and their parlance, their diction and their sense of humour. They listen to things that nobody else was ever meant to hear, and they translate it — not just from one language into another, but also in the sense of meaning and tone and significance. Their translations are one of the many cogs in the machine of British intelligence, informing and guiding a broader picture of a target or a threat. What they hear and how they translate it can escalate an overlooked conversation into a threat to national security. The way they listen can demarcate the difference between life and death.

We sit on either side of a large table in a room with no windows, and everyone lays their notebooks on the table the same way people would their phones, if they had them. It is one of the most formal interviews I've ever undertaken. We walk through my questions, talk about their earliest memories of listening (both recall lullabies; Jill's the American folk songs her dad would sing to her, Tia the Sylheti and Arabic prayers her grandmother would lull her to sleep with) and what languages meant to them at school. They both uncovered their linguistic dexterity differently: Jill was raised in a solely English-speaking family but was 'constantly trying to find new ways of getting involved in language' as a child, 'hassling [her school] to let me do more languages', while Tia, who cites growing up around Bollywood films as an influence on her linguistic aptitude, only started to learn languages formally at GCHQ, after completing her legal training, 'hating' law and needing a job.

Jill trained as an interpreter before joining GCHQ. 'I think that really changed the way I listened,' she tells me. She did work experience at the UN. There, she sat in one of the silent interpreter booths, practising to take her simultaneous interpreting course. 'It's the hardest type of interpretation,' she explains, 'listening to someone speaking, translating it in your head and saying the other language out loud at the same time. The time lag can't be too long because you can get too behind, and then you're thinking too much about what you're saying, then the stuff you're listening to stops going into your head. But it can't be too short either, because you have to deal with those chunks of meaning. If you don't get to the end of a chunk of meaning, you might end up saying absolutely the wrong thing.' She cites an instance of a translator wrongly introducing the delegate from the United Kingdom as one from the United States. 'That wrong answer stuck with me, because for the listener – the consumer of this interpreting – they're going to think that that interpreter didn't know the difference between Britain and America. And that seems like a really silly mistake. But actually, when you are having to anticipate and get those chunks of meaning in quickly, it's such an easy thing to do.' It left her brain, she says, trained in the ability to listen, think and process simultaneously.

While training at GCHQ, Tia says she was resistant to the traditional teaching of languages as broken down into their composite chunks. 'I said to my teachers from the start that I don't get on with grammar. I don't understand it, it's too directional and boxy.' When they asked how she learned, Tia said, 'By listening to how people speak differently: give me a phrase and give me ten different ways of you saying it. I don't know why my brain works that way, but that's how I understand it.' She started to learn Punjabi: 'I didn't think I had a particular aptitude for it; what I did learn was that through knowing Sylheti, Bengali and other Asian languages, I could fit it together and understand it.'

There is a tacit understanding that the linguists can only tell me so much: I am not here to learn the gristly details of intelligence operations or uncover sensitive material. Instead, I want to find out how these women listen, how they have learned to listen, how their listening differs from the kind that isn't responsible for locating international threat and whether I can deepen my own as a result. Still, I can't resist asking for examples of when their work made a notable impact.

'I have a few instances from across my career, but the one that I go to happened when I was eight months into the job,' replies Tia. 'I was listening to something. At first, I thought it was a normal conversation, but then I homed in and realised it wasn't. I heard something crucial, and I insisted to my seniors that it needed to be escalated.' Tia, despite being so new in the role, insisted that the analyst she reported to rewrite their report: 'They hadn't conveyed what I had heard.' She offered up a verbatim script, 'with all of my context', rather than a more condensed translation – 'to emphasise the seriousness of it'. Still, the subsequent report didn't capture what she was trying to convey. 'It went to someone even more senior, and he came to me and said: "We've changed the report three times, and you still aren't happy. What is it?" So I told him and he got it, and he wrote the report verbatim with the context and audio cues I'd heard, without interpreting it into something else. What I'd heard was too important for someone not to include it, or to put their own stance into it. It had to go in the report. If you just looked at the raw, written-down version of the words, without the context I was providing, it may have seemed like it said something else, or meant something else. It would have missed that crucial something. And it did have real-world consequences, and I knew it would have real-world consequences when I was hearing it. I knew it had to be escalated.'

The reason Tia knew it was important was the same reason it was so easily overlooked: 'It wasn't about what was being said, it was about who was speaking, and who those people were. To anyone else listening, they would have thought it was two ordinary people. But not if you knew who they were.' Tia was conscious that one of the people had access to sensitive information; her listening, her ability to translate what she was hearing, gave her an insight that others couldn't comprehend.

'We do a lot of checking,' says Jill. 'You get people saying, "Well, it can't possibly be this thing, because it wouldn't make any sense." And then you go back and say, "Well, it would make sense if you've noticed that they sort of laugh a little bit after they've said it," or it's the thing that they said before they kind of cut off slightly in the middle of a sentence – that shows they're rephrasing. It's not like the two things they said were contradictory, it's that they misspoke the first time.' She gives an example where she was checking the translation that a colleague had done. In it, they had used a familiar piece of vocabulary that Jill felt 'didn't quite work'. 'There was something about the inflection of the way it was said,' she said. Instead, Jill thought, the speaker was using a different word — a colloquial one, one she'd never heard before, 'but I thought from the way the person said it, and from the definitions of the word, that it was this other word.' It was a risk, she says, to put it to her colleague with the admission that she didn't know the word either. But it paid off: 'Six months later, from a completely different route, what I was working on ended up on the news, and the word I'd heard was reported. It was what I thought it was — I'd got it right.'

The linguists at GCHQ are listening for things that other people simply don't know how to hear: inflection, tone, the difference between speakers, strange slang, the things that are half-said and the things not said at all. All these hidden meanings, these smallest of clues, which carry unthinkable significance. 'You're the one that's listening, not the intelligence analyst,' says Tia. 'The analyst relies on your translated interpretation of the situation. You have to get it absolutely spot on. There's no room for misunderstanding in terms of what you're trying to convey to your analyst, because it's in a foreign language and they're not listening to it raw, as you are. You know there could be real-life consequences and the responsibility is on you, you feel it. To make sure that you get it right.'

'Translating a foreign language for someone is a communicative act,' Jill adds. 'It's really important that you know as much about what you're listening to, but also that you know as much as you can about your own knowledge, your own biases, and that you also know the people that you're translating for, what they're likely to understand and what they're not likely to understand.' Their translation acts as a key: they have to know the mechanism of the lock as well as they do the door. And instances like that which Jill cites, where she sees her decisions reported on the news, are once-in-a-career rare: 'Most of what we do is so sensitive. Often you just can't know. You might never really know if you made the right call or not. And sometimes there can be so much riding on the call that you make, that's why you have to be super clear and really open to new information. You have to be scientific about it.'

The way Jill and Tia speak about how they listen makes it sound expansive, I tell them. 'I think it is useful to not be too linear in how you listen,' Jill says; to acknowledge that only understanding some of what you've heard isn't a failure but a beginning. She often cites translation as being like a puzzle to solve – 'putting your native language and another language side by side and working out what goes straight through and what doesn't, negotiating that gap and negotiating the dissonance' – rather than a test to get immediately right. Context, both linguists tell me, is as crucial as the words that are being said. Often, they are conveying meaning from a recording that nobody knows better than them: 'You could be the only person who's been constantly listening to that piece, or if you've listened to the speaker at a different point in time, you might get to know when they're being sarcastic, or when they're being serious, or when they're admitting and saying something so you know that they know about it. Those kind of things make you sit up and think, "That's interesting,"' Tia says. That example she gave, when she was new in the job, was one of many that was reliant on context: 'I had this enormous sense that it needed to go out accurate, with all the emotions I could hear properly conveyed, because without the emotion, you're just reading words on a page without context. You don't actually get it.'

Jill emphasises: 'In our world, for example, you could have the intelligence saying: "Person X, clearly irritated, said . . ." and "Person Y, clearly calm, said . . .". They could be saying the same thing, but picking up their manner is huge, because the decision tree at GCHQ could go off either way, depending on which of those it is.' Making that choice, she adds, is in keying into how people communicate and bringing those expectations into your understanding even as you're trying to challenge them. 'When people talk, they tend to speak quite predictably,' Jill explains. 'If you start a certain phrase, it'll nearly always end in a few different ways. Being able to anticipate what those few most likely options are, then rule a few or all of them out – and realising when you got your anticipation wrong – is a big part of the skill, because if you try to approach every syllable as it comes, and try to fit possible words to every syllable, then you get stuck really quickly. Especially because sometimes the audio quality is poor, and so you are literally not hearing the thing that was said originally.'

This is listening that happens on several layers: that of focus and analysis but also of anticipation and context. Of filling in the blanks when the blanks could be gravely important. The linguists listen in a way that is three-dimensional: not simply down the end of a headphone wire, but with knowledge and experience and questioning. An aural riddle to solve that could curb disaster. It's a listening rich with contradiction because it has to be; both women speak of solving problems by using a physicality that extends beyond their brain; that they inherently knew to push for a correction, or that they had a gut feeling – even though, as Jill says, 'a gut feeling can't always go into something as evidence.'

I ask if their training has melted into their experience of the outside world and they speak, light-heartedly, of their hearing in a way I'd imagine someone with super-powers might. 'When I'm out and about, if someone's having a conversation – from across a cafe – I can hear it and tune in, which can be entertaining sometimes,' Tia says with a wry smile. 'I can cut out the other background noise and focus in. Recently I went to a coffee shop with a friend and I saw a couple having what looked to be their first date – and I love [the TV show] *First Dates* – and I could just focus in on listening, even though my friend and I were still having a conversation.'

Jill laughs, says she can do that too: 'I'm not sure when that happened, I just have that ability to focus.' It reminds me of what those who knew Pauline Oliveros said about her, how she could switch from cracking a joke to listening deeply in a matter of seconds. And it's seemingly one of those skills that emerges among those who work in the world of professional listeners: Jill mentions watching, agog, as an interpreter for the UN performed an 'extremely technical simultaneous interpretation of a highly technical speech' while doing her make-up: 'She put her brain onto autopilot.' Tia cites the little legend of linguists so adept at decoding Morse code they could 'listen to Morse in one ear, and Test Match Special in the other'.

What, I ask the women, would they impart to those who want to become better listeners? Their answers are stripped-back and simple in comparison to what we've recently been discussing. Simple, if enormous: 'Patience,' says Tia. 'So you can be in the moment and focus. But you need to have empathy. And reading between the lines can be important. Having some sort of compassion as well. I think those things intertwine into how you become a more attentive listener.' It's worth noting that during our conversation neither of the women speak over one another once. Jill echoes this in her answer, citing thinking while listening but also giving space. 'That ability to analyse while you're listening can help you to really take a step back, and instead of reacting to what you've just heard, think about what they're actually trying to get across to you. Focusing on the words but being able to draw back from the words and tell the story behind the words. The rigour around not misrepresenting or inserting ourselves unconsciously into what we're doing. There's real empathy we develop through the listening work that we do.'

Our time is up; the linguists must return to their work. We shuffle out of the windowless room and into the open-plan offices, where the same recycling bins and posters about workplace initiatives dot the landscape as if this were any other nine-to-five. My contact goes ahead, tells people that I'm about to walk through – they must pause what they're talking about for a few seconds – and soon I am back with the smart, genial men, collecting all of my switched-off electronics.

It takes a while for the conversation I've had with Jill and Tia to sink in. Usually I record the interviews I do with people, and, in the weeks and months after, I go over those recordings. When I do, I listen for new meanings. I run over inaudible moments repeatedly to make sure I have understood what has been said. I am no intelligence analyst, there is a different kind of sensitivity to my work, but I am familiar with the actions of listening to a conversation and dredging meaning from it.

The security measures at GCHQ meant that the only recording of our conversation was undertaken by the contact who accompanied me to the interview; he transcribed our conversation from it, and weeks after we meet I receive the transcript. When I read it back, I am transported to the moment when the three of us spoke – to the table, to the colour of the lanyard around Jill's neck and the way the women were sitting, what they had used to write in their notebooks before our meeting. But I still wonder what a recording of our conversation may have held; whether I really did ask my questions as clearly as the record states, whether Jill and Tia responded exactly as is written. Any differences would be too small to be perceptible, but if I have learned anything from meeting these women, it is that the imperceptible differences make the difference.

My work does not save lives, but every day I keep a small child alive. Every day I keep a small child alive and most days I contemplate his death; check the monitor for sounds of him breathing, to watch if his chest rises and falls. I have sat in hospital wards and only afterwards learned how close he was to not living. Since he was born, since I first heard his heartbeat, my body has started to wire itself into a new way of understanding – understanding sound, understanding touch, understanding risk and safety – and I have learned to translate these inputs as much as I have been frustrated by my incomprehension of them.

Somewhere between the sleep-deprived synapses of my brain and the incorrigible stubbornness of my gut I have become a creature who can tell when my child is hungry or tired or uncomfortable. This takes patience and empathy and the ability to think and process while listening. To make sense of something when it doesn't add up, when a syllable is missing or the sounds are inaudible.

I am fascinated by Jill and Tia's work, by the expertise they have built up and worked so hard to achieve; I'll never know quite what dangers they have spared us, none of us will. This is listening on another level entirely. But I am beginning to learn that I am better connected to sound than I ever realised; that I am plugged into something that is crucial and demanding and valuable – even if it is rarely valued. Like the work of the linguists at GCHQ, so much of the sound we translate goes unheard. We are just another woman on another bus with a crying baby, trying to comfort them.

BRIDGES

A THIN, ADULT BODY EMERGES from a door at the side of the warehouse; their long fingers and palms are covered in black dust. Spidery tattoos interrupt stretches of their pale skin. We – me, a couple of other people who have turned up to this small gallery space in South London on a Saturday morning for a 16-minute-long performance – can't see the top of their face; it's covered by a plaster-cast mask that is attached to their hand. The body is miming to a libretto spoken by children. The verse spills out in trickles and putters, like water, and the person moves with childlike caution and playfulness, stretching up onto tiptoes, crouching down in fear. 'Big dreams are made in parts and carefully,' they tell us. It's a captivating sight, to witness a little voice seemingly come out of a grown body. While I logically know that the performer is miming, as the piece continues I find myself both believing and not at the same time: the performer is the children; the performer is an adult miming along to a recording of children. Both things are true. A child sounds different when their voice is given over to an adult.

The performance has been made by Fani Parali, a Greek artist whose work I encountered at a show in a different city a few weeks earlier. There, in another old industrial building, Fani had made an incubator out of steel bars. Inside lay a tender pencil drawing of a newborn baby on a cushion, his toes dwarfed by a name tag around his foot, his eyes blinded by bandages, a heart rate monitor stuck to his chest, a feeding tube, an arm bandaged from palm to elbow, a tube sticking out of it. Above the drawing, a speaker was hung. To stand above the incubator was to hear a composition that Fani had made from recordings she had taken while her son spent the first month of his life in neonatal intensive care. You can hear his tiny bleats and a woman's voice tenderly echoing them, a kind of looping coo. You can hear stretches of quiet when only the bleeping hospital machines drift down over the sculpture. After I saw this work, placed in the middle of a room painted red, alongside pieces considering motherhood and creation from a collection of female artists, I kept going back to it. There was an intimacy and a poignancy to it that is almost too much to bear, but nevertheless reeled me in. The baby is anonymised by the apparatus that is keeping him alive, but he is also recognisable by his vulnerability: only someone very close to him, only someone who had birthed him, could have depicted him in this way.

'When I made it, I truly felt that I had to make this work, that it had to come out,' she tells me later. 'It was a way of understanding for me. It was like an archive of that moment.' Geographically, Fani and I are barely a mile apart, but we're speaking on Zoom because the only time we can find to speak is in the evening. Matt is out and I must stay in with the baby. Fani is sitting in her car, parked in a pretty Georgian square near a park, letting her partner navigate bedtime with their now-toddler. We speak with the efficiency and warmth of mothers with young children at the end of a day that started many hours before: diving deep quickly, wasting no time with small talk. As an artist, Fani has built sound into her practice since she was studying at the Royal Academy. While she draws and makes sculptures, often from steel and medical gauze – materials that manage to convey both strength and vulnerability – she has also written scripts or librettos for people to record that other people, often drag artists, then embody through lip-synching. It's important, she tells me, that the parts are not acted out: 'There was something about the recorded voice; you get all these incredible little nuances and breaths and glitches and pauses.' In separating voice and body, and then bringing them back together again 'in a heightened state',

Fani realised she could share those most intimate of things: inner monologues, fears, longings.

I hold on to Jill and Tia's advice in the weeks and months after I meet with them. In particular, I hang on to the notions of empathy and patience, two things I try my best to pour out to my son but have little of left over for myself. While the flashbacks have stilled and my thinking is more cogent, some days I am still caught out by the remnants of PTSD. I come to realise that, in the midst of all this listening, all this thinking about listening, I have overlooked the need to listen to myself. It will take empathy and patience to hear her, the woman I am now, and it will need context and paying attention to the gaps between the words. It feels like work, but it's work that has to be done if I'm to emerge from the noise.

Listening has always tied Fani to her loved ones – not always in easy ways. Her father died when she was twelve. Several years afterwards she heard his voice on a tape. 'I was in shock, because it just brought him back. I just felt he was there. It was so much more powerful than his image, like a picture, or my memory.' One of her sisters, who died in the months before we speak, was an alcoholic and Fani explains that she had 'seen her in states where I couldn't communicate with her, and also when she would try and mutter things but it was impossible to understand. These are all things that have affected me. I've always held this notion of voice as an entity, as a very important thing, and tried to put bridges in where there aren't.' Ever since starting her art practice a decade ago, Fani has been preoccupied with the in-between; of absence and presence, of receiving and giving: 'How do we bring something that is not close to us, close to us?' When her son was born with a medical issue that necessitated surgery when he was five days old, it felt like a lot of what she had been thinking about was tweaked to fever-pitch: 'I was talking about care, about how do you get close to someone if you're not physically there, how can you communicate on a deep level? And suddenly I'm confronted with this?'

Fani's son was so small and so unwell that he spent most of his time in the incubator: initially, she was only able to hold him for a few minutes at a time. He couldn't be breastfed, and so was sustained through a feeding tube; Fani and her partner would frequently discuss his hunger with the medical staff looking after him. Often, she and his father would sing to him – these sounds are among those that radiate out above *Incubator* – and, Fani says, this became a kind of replacement for touch: 'Singing became so important because it brought us connection. It was our sounds that became the bridge while he was in the incubator.' There were also the non-human noises, those of the machines. 'I will never forget those sounds, those bleeping alarms,' she explains. 'Those sounds became this strange tune of his recovery. Those little bleeps, for their heart rates or their temperatures, that count life. What a crazy thing, so vital and unbearable at the same time.' I feel deeply fortunate to never have experienced NICU; even when I walked past its door on the way to my son's ward months before, I felt that gratitude. But I knew a little of what Fani was speaking of, that strange dependency on the noises of the machines measuring your baby's existence, these mechanical songs of hope, deep fear and survival.

While Fani and her partner would spend their days in NICU, they had to rest at night. 'So that's when we left him. The NICU was always quieter then, so we thought maybe if we left in those hours, we could be with him all day,' she explains. 'But there was this insane distance between us and this new tiny baby. All you want to do is hold them, make sure they're okay, and you can't do that.' I ask her how those nights were, how that absence manifested for her, and she pauses. 'The anomaly of not being able to hear him every second was so powerful,' she says. 'The sound was really hard. If I heard him cry but I couldn't see him, it was unbearable. I couldn't actually think about it too much, his cry. That's all he would have done that month, those little cries, because he wasn't making more elaborate sounds then.

'I'm not sure if I've ever thought about it like this, but I think it was my absence to him, that's more what I thought about. That I was absent, forcefully. It haunts me to this day, obviously. It's always going to haunt me.'

I suspect Fani's phone is rested on the dashboard; her camera is tilted slightly up at her, and from my desk I watch her play with her hair as she lets me in on some of the most traumatic moments of her life. As she gesticulates, her red fingernails interrupt the side of the screen. Inside this everyday cocoon of the car we talk about the things only parents of hospitalised babies are familiar with: the noises in the ward, the strange vacuum that arises once they are discharged, the lapse between the event unfolding and the realisation of trauma manifesting in your body, being told by a GP to seek support because nobody else has quite found the words yet. I feel so seen by her; there is such surprising relief in talking about these difficult things in so knowing a way.

Fani's son was less than a year old when she was commissioned to make a piece for a show that involved sound. We talk about the peculiar sounds that people make when trying to communicate with babies; the animalistic call-and-refrain of wordless noises, some of which are played through *Incubator*. As an artist whose work had played with the power of sound to slow down and fragment time, who understood the power of a voice – not only as something that is spoken, but as something that exists in another capacity when it is heard – she was able to reframe the weeks she spent mothering her son through the challenges of intensive care by the recordings she had made of him. Fani used videos and recordings of her child that existed for the same reason that anybody else takes videos of their newborn baby – 'I was just desperately trying to keep hold of his presence' – it was just that hers happened to have hospital alarms in the background. 'I think maybe subconsciously I did know that I needed to keep moments. I wasn't able to filter things back then because I was in such a kind of shock.'

When I ask Fani about listening, she talks about care. 'I've found I've had to learn a whole other way of listening, especially with my sister, when she's not been well or in times of crisis. It's a listening not only for what the person is saying, but with a lot more nuance. There's a beautiful Greek word – αφουγκράζομαι – which means listening with my whole body, or in a heightened state. It's about the receiving but also being, in order to then give back.'

And so, Fani drew her son in pencil. She made an incubator from steel rods – 'A life-saving machine and a cage at the same time. What my baby needs to survive, and also what is keeping me from him.' She laid sounds of her singing over recordings of her son's smallest noises: 'Those first primal sounds. I wanted to bring this effect of what a voice and a sound does on a deeper level, one that can't be intellectually analysed, but one that kind of hits you.'

Speaking now, 18 months after *Incubator* first went on display, Fani says she never foresaw the future of the work – so much of its existence arrived because it gave her a means of connection to those weeks when her son was so unwell. But its appearance in the group show – which opened in Bristol, where I saw it, but will go on to tour the country for the next 15 months – was something she couldn't have envisaged. She says it's been moving to have encountered people who have found connection through the piece. She mentions a conversation she had with someone who had also spent his first months of life in intensive care, who felt the piece honoured his mother who insisted doctors take her hunch that her child was unwell seriously. Fani was looking around the show alone, the morning after the hubbub of the opening, when she spoke with an invigilator at the gallery who introduced himself as 'an incubator baby'. 'He said he found it hard to sit next to the work but that he was managing a little more time each day,' she explains. 'He told me: "I'm never able to talk about this."' People don't, she says; they don't know how to navigate those conversations around unwell children or the times when they were in intensive care. It echoes with me: people were so understandably insistent on celebrating my son's recovery that his illness shrank in comparison. In the process, I was left wondering why it had left me so unhinged. In making a work that reconnects the sound and imagery of the first few weeks of her matrescence and her son's existence, Fani has forged a bridge of her own: one that other people with similar experiences are able to use to process and communicate through. It's something she's still trying to make sense of, she says: 'Little things happen that are so meaningful and, I don't know, maybe the fear and the trauma are shared for a second.'

This was another kind of translation: a connection, a bridge, between one person's unspeakable experience and another. Difficult things swell in silence, but listening – whether down a phone line or across a stretch of South London or in person, by chance, at an exhibition – lets them breathe. This was patience and empathy encapsulated in a sculpture in an exhibition, and it struck me that creating it was, for Fani, perhaps an act of empathy and patience. How else to cope with noises we wish we hadn't heard, than by taking hold of them and making something that allows us to listen more deeply to them?

Now that the bridge was there – in *Incubator* and among those who saw it, but also in the conversation that Fani and I had as a result – people could cross it. We were bound together by this communal listening; I had been granted access to what some of the most difficult moments of her life had sounded like. For so long I had felt alone in my listening, but speaking with Fani made me realise that I was part of a larger body of women tuning in – from Annea in the water, and Claire, who picked up our childhood friendship, to Jane and Jenny, who shared their ways of listening with me, and now Fani. Perhaps this had always been a kind of song I was trying to piece together. Perhaps we were always listening alongside one another.

Late Winter

I THROW A QUILT ON the kitchen floor and lay the baby down on it. We have been out for most of the day. Drizzly weather, with enough low light in the sky to warrant an electric bulb, I suddenly want to be inside and I want to cook.

The baby is squeaking, something he does when he is bored or uncomfortable. He's old enough now to sense when I am more engaged by something that isn't him. I chatter to him while I open the cupboard and pull out an onion, push the door to with my foot, pull on the fridge door. Peppers, celery, garlic. Oils seized from another cupboard. I whip my phone out of my pocket, find *Tapestry* by Carole King and load it up to play through the speaker. The baby's head turns at the first thundering chord of 'I Feel The Earth Move'. I dance and sing along, a bizarre private performance just for him. He quietens and watches me. I have bought enough time to chop one vegetable.

The baby stills when I sing. It happens in the car when he is angry; it happens when he is calm but bored. After watching the faint blue cross appear on the pregnancy test, it took me four days and a realisation of what song I would sing to him – 'We Almost Had A Baby' by Emmy the Great – to acknowledge that I was carrying something other than myself. Now he's here I sing to him constantly, always have done. I sing the songs my mother sang to me ('Space Oddity' by David Bowie), I sing ones I have made up ('Naked Baby'). My repertoire is small and peculiar. Taylor Swift's 'Lover' is in there, but Jeff Buckley's 'Lover, You Should've Come Over' is not. When he was 13 weeks old I learned all the words to Imogen Heap's baby-mesmerising 'The Happy Song'. I will sing this song with no embarrassment in public – often on buses – for months to come.

I pass the hours cycling through nursery staples I've collected from children's centres. On the morning I cried in the waiting room, I walked home with 'Zoom, Zoom, Zoom, We're Going To The Moon' rolling around my head. I pushed the buggy along the potholed pavement, my son's sleeping skull lying back in his sling, and wondered if I looked as deranged as I felt, with unbrushed hair and pink eyes and a stare that a friend had described as 'brain-dead' 48 hours earlier. 'Zoom, zoom, zoom! We'll be there very soon!': a soundtrack to the start of a PTSD and postnatal anxiety diagnosis, the baby's sweet-sour medicine breath drifting into my face. Going to the moon. At times I felt like this made more sense, as if I were looking out at the world from behind a thick pane of glass.

But this is a better day, this is a day for kitchen music. As the bassline of 'It's Too Late' smoothly walks across the room, I toss celery, onion and garlic into a pan of warming oil. I croon at the baby, who rolls between my ankles. I'm here, but I'm also in the kitchen of my adolescence, occupying my mother's space. She loved this album long before I did, one among the millions of King fans who sent it to the top of the Billboard charts for five weeks in 1971. I found my own way with it when I was 12, my pre-teen heart softened for the unconditional love and minor-key bridge of 'You've Got a Friend'. I've cycled back to *Tapestry* countless times since, nearly always alone. For me, it's a solitude record – apart from when I stood next to my mother and watched King play it in its entirety in Hyde Park, one heartbroken summer – perhaps because of the intimacy of the arenas in which I always listen to it: kitchens, bedrooms, sometimes the car.

It takes on new meaning as I add more ingredients to the pan, notice the steam gathering above the hob. This – this grey Thursday afternoon that has come with a craving to melt down vegetables into a sweet, salty, acid brew – is the first time I've played *Tapestry* since having the baby. I am inhabiting what my mother's actions taught me by doing: feeding a crowd on the remnants of the fridge, gently showing her children the shape of her daily domestic work, making space for herself through music. In this moment, as I absent-mindedly toss in salt and vinegar, sing to the baby and rub his gurgling stomach, I am both in the kitchen of my childhood and the one I am making for my own child. I am here because of a record, because of the familiar beats and peaks and troughs of melody. Music has woven the two together and made something new in the process.

DELPHI

'I MEAN, THE SOUND THAT I found really profound was the first time I heard Delphi's heartbeat,' Natasha Khan tells me. We're in her kitchen in East London, seated on either side of a small wooden table. Delphi is her daughter. Natasha is telling me about something that happened five years earlier, when she was early in her pregnancy and went to visit a midwife, Nancy, a 'silver-haired, beautiful woman in her sixties who had helped to birth 1,500 babies'. She'd not expected to hear a heartbeat that day, but Nancy had the equipment and asked if she wanted to. 'And she was looking for a while, and there was nothing. She said, "Oh, they don't like the sound waves, they move away from it, even if they're tiny. Don't worry, we'll find it." And then suddenly there was just, like, a magical sound.'

I ask if it surprised her, what it sounded like. 'It was much faster than I imagined. And because you see it all the time in movies and people talk about it so much, it's supposed to be emotional. But I suppose until you actually hear it . . . It's different when it's your baby.'

Natasha is a musician, among other things. When we speak, she is working on a novel, has recently created a tarot deck and is weeks away from releasing her sixth album, *The Dream of Delphi*. It was news of this record that had prompted me to contact her: Natasha had published a mission statement when she announced the new album, and in it I found a kind of mirror to the year I'd been living. In the wake of having a child, she wrote, 'I returned momentarily to the cycles and seasons, through naps and breastfeeds, writing this music in any spare moment I could, methodically mapping out the experience of having my mind slowly blown by something so seemingly common.'

Becoming a mother, Natasha's statement continued, made her realise how damaged the human connection with nature was; how the increasingly urban, capitalist and digital nature of human existence had placed us 'in the hands of something that's very lifeless'. It speaks of mother archetypes — of crones and sages and witches and midwifes — and how distant they feel; of a need to 'heal our society' by 'reconnect[ing] with our empathy, compassion, power and love, which to me is a very matriarchal energy'. The album, the statement continues, 'is just my tiny way of trying to reconnect people . . . a small slice of music, about a very personal story, and I made it for Delphi so she can hear it when she's grown and know how much her mum loved her.'

I found some of the statement challenging – perhaps in its enormity, perhaps in the pedestals upon which it puts the matters of undefinable things, such as energy and archetypes. But I was intrigued nevertheless. As Bat for Lashes, the alias under which Natasha has earned three Mercury Prize nominations and Ivor Novello awards and released Top 10 albums, Natasha represented a part of my life I felt I had left behind. A time when I was actively clamouring to be a music journalist, reviewing gigs and devouring promo CDs and working out how to fit into a world that operated from behind barriers, and a time when I felt it all slipping away, my disconnection shifting into new realms of quietude. Even speaking with a musician about sound and listening was slightly uncomfortable for me; I felt the shame and imposter syndrome that had accompanied me when I was writing about music rear up. I had begun this journey with an intention to listen more deeply, to reconnect with the music that had defined so much of my life. More than two years later and I still wasn't putting on many more records than I had then; I wasn't aware of what songs were in the charts; I couldn't recognise the pop stars in the adverts on the Tube. My life still felt divorced from that entire realm of sound, but I no longer felt diminished by it, no longer believed my existence to be muffled as a result. Instead, I was acutely aware of the sounds that made up my life, of what it was to tune in and acknowledge them. In veering off my original course, I realised that it had been a direct journey across an expanse that held so much more besides music: the noises made by life, and the sounds that living was made of.

When I told people about these things – this kind of aural ephemera – I described them as ambiguous, as the lived experiences that defied categorisation or, often, recognition. Some more so than others: phantom crying, for instance, is both real and imagined. But others were easier to recognise and merely overlooked. Often, these were noises associated with women's lives, of 'chatter' and crying babies. Perhaps I found Natasha's statement, the creative impetus behind *The Dream of Delphi*, so alluring because it seemed dedicated to a belief that our existence was lacking because we dismissed feminine power. Perhaps I found it daunting because I had to learn how not to dismiss it, and dismiss my own alongside it, too.

There are ten tracks on *The Dream of Delphi*. I listen to them in snatches – on public transport, during the short walk to pick the baby up from nursery, in the kitchen while I cook. It's a record that feels both feather-light and plummeting at the same time, and it takes me a while to tune into it. After a few listens ahead of meeting Natasha, I stop; the stream runs out of access time and I neglect to renew it. I stay put in a life without music.

Natasha found out she was pregnant in the toilets backstage ahead of the penultimate show of her 2019 tour ('I was so out of my body; you have this special sort of twinkling secret'). Four months later the world started to lock down in response to Covid. She was living in Los Angeles and had already begun to navigate her pregnancy as a creative project on its own terms. 'It was such an interesting moment, to have a baby in the middle of lockdown,' she explains. 'Everything just went quiet, yet my body – tuning into internal sounds or feelings or vibrations, or just natural sounds – had the space to heighten, and was already heightening anyway because I was pregnant. The world stopped and got quieter and the animal side of me grew.' Natasha tells me that, in labour, she sounded 'like a groaning cow', a sound that 'was coming from the depths of the earth, it felt like'.

Delphi was born at home, and when I ask Natasha about her sonic memories of her daughter's arrival, it's not the newborn noises she remembers, but the silence. She paints me a scene in the hours after birth: she's in bed with tea and toast and tiny, newborn Delphi, looking out at glass doors that lead onto a porch. 'I remember looking out and just seeing this weird twilight time. The midwives left, and [my partner] and Delphi fell asleep. I felt like it was this liminal space where everything was silent. It was this silent world between worlds: I wasn't not a mother, and I wasn't a mother yet.

'I was in this threshold moment and everyone else had gone and I felt this existential loneliness, like I was in a spotlight standing in the world. It was a moment that was unrepeatable; it was a moment, and I was just lying. I felt like I'd been in a war, but I was also so aware of this peace after so much motion and noise and movement. It was that silent it was almost like this huge tear in the fabric of reality; I was just completely washed clean of everything for a minute. I felt the mirage of existence had fallen away, and this real sense of connection to animals and plants: that every living thing goes through this process of death and rebirth and birth and growing and dying. I was just overwhelmed with the serenity of that feeling.' Natasha says she fell asleep afterwards and awoke to the sun rising, bringing with it a sense of 'pure joy: it was over'.

These hours are represented by two songs on *The Dream of Delphi*: 'The Midwifes Have Left' and 'Her First Morning'. The former is spare and spectral, wordless vocal chords folded atop gently building piano keys like origami. The latter is more euphoric; Natasha's cooing vocals sound a little more sure, they're tentatively growing into something, reaching out into a new kind of existence. 'It was really interesting trying to make music around that experience,' says Natasha. 'Initially I didn't want to do any lyrics because I couldn't really put words to the feelings I was having; the lyrics ended up being just little fragments. It's just a fraction of my small human ability to put music to the thing.'

Matrescence changed sound for Natasha, a person who has been engaged with making noise as a musician and a vocalist for most of her life. Years ago, before Delphi, she got 'really obsessed with going on night walks without a torch because I wanted my ears to turn on. I wanted to absorb everything.' But there was 'something about pregnancy that made me continuously connected to something beyond myself'. Once Delphi was born Natasha noticed that her 'ears just went insane. At the slightest shifting in her cot I would sit up. What I found interesting was I was totally overtaken by this instinct that was beyond my control. Any slightest hiccup or gurgle or breath. It's not just your ears that are hearing it, it's your whole body that senses their whole body; there's an interchange between our vibrational expressions.' I'm reminded, I tell her, of the raw first days after I gave birth, when I would lie awake despite bone-shattering exhaustion and listen to the strange dialogue between my husband's sleeping breath and the baby's fluttering exhales. 'Motherhood drags you down into a state that we would all be in if we were living in greater connection with nature and less artificial environments,' she says. 'I think that's why it's been such a profound spiritual awakening for me, because as a child I was so naturally connected. There's been this never-ending longing and melancholy towards wanting to keep that thread alive.'

Having been astonished by where motherhood has taken her spiritually, Natasha believes society doesn't offer people enough space to properly occupy it: 'It's a moment to be quiet and I think that women aren't allowed that big space around having a baby; it should be, like, a year and a half, to really marinate in that experience. We're sort of forced back out way too quickly.'

Hours pass. I leave the intimacy of Natasha's home – kitten playing on the floor, Polaroids on the fridge, little shoes lined up by the door – and head back across London. It feels like a lot of what I've been thinking about – the tussle between artificial, digital noise and the sounds of the outside, organic world; the strange metamorphosis my senses have undergone during my matrescence and how the space I occupy has changed since – has been thrown up by our conversation. I feel seen, but I've also had my thinking challenged. I admire the way Natasha is able to inhabit, to embrace, her matrescence and her motherhood so fully. Perhaps in three years' time, when my son is the same age that Delphi is now, I will too. Right now, it still feels as if I am emerging from something and the outside world is not quite ready for it; that I am not quite ready for it, that I am still made of tissue-paper layers: who I was, who I am, who I will be. That in listening to myself I must also accept who I am, who I am becoming, who I have lost. It is still easier for me to tune into the sounds of what society expects mothers to be, rather than that more vivid and vital song of what kind of mother I am.

When Beloved sings in Toni Morrison's novel of the same name, it changes things for the women in her family. It comes after Sethe, Denver and Beloved have had a rare good day; they go ice skating, they use their bodies, they laugh until they cough and cry. 'Three notes; before the melody was even clear. Leaning forward a little, Beloved was humming softly.' It comes before what Morrison describes as 'the click – the settling of pieces into places designed and made especially for them'. Sethe can't, in that moment, conflate the physicality of the woman next to her and the toddler she murdered out of love, but 'the click had clicked; things were where they ought to be', and it was song that did it: '"I made that song up," said Sethe. "I made it up and sang it to my children. Nobody knows that song but me and my children."' Beloved knows it. And it offers them freedom: there is a new quiet, no more from 'the voices that ringed 124 like a noose'. Instead, 'the women inside were free at last to be what they liked, see whatever they saw and say whatever was on their minds'. Throughout *Beloved*, words are difficult things – stories can't be told, memories remain unspeakable – but sound and song offers a resolution and a reclamation to a motherhood that has been haunted. When the community of neighbouring women return to 124 and to Sethe after 18 years of condemnation, they sing, searching 'for the right combination, the key, the code, the sound that broke the back of words. Building voice upon voice until they found it, and when they did it was a wave of sound wide enough to sound deep water and knock the pods off chestnut trees. It broke over Sethe and she trembled like the baptized in its wash.' The song breaks the spell between Sethe and Beloved.

A few weeks after meeting Natasha I listen to *The Dream of Delphi* again. I put the album on and I turn my attention for everything else off – my phone, my inbox, my computer screen, the constant patter of thoughts in my head. I haven't sat and listened to music in this way for so long: at least a decade. And it is so different from before, when I was trying to listen alongside the other parts of my day. I have made space. I don't allow a critical response in, I stop the near-mechanical cogs that try to assess the album's merit, to question how it hangs together as a record or to ask what it's saying or doing or even what it sounds like. I close my eyes. I let the music in. The last of an incense stick curls into smoke in the air. I wonder if my brain is also building new connections in the process. I think about the rituals of listening, of how absent they are in my life. I feel self-conscious in creating this kind of ceremony but I push through into a space where I can just be with this music. I feel my body soften and my breathing slow. I find myself constricted by the chair and unfurl the headphone cable so I can lie down instead. I stare up at the ceiling; I look out through the window, take in the new spring leaves on the neighbour's tree outside, a tree I so rarely consider let alone look at. I watch the sunlight catch in the feathery fronds of fennel. The music – this music, this album Natasha made for her daughter – heightens everything. My chest heaves and my hands come to my face and I am sobbing into them, and I realise that this is the first time in a year that I am crying not with exhaustion or overwhelm or sadness but with something deeper, something more inexplicable. This is a release akin to the tidal wave I felt when I heard my son's heartbeat for the first time. It's a connection.

I sit with the album until it is finished, and it feels like it has evaporated into time; 40 minutes pass in nothing at all. The sounds of it are sumptuous: layered, synth-laden vocals and bold brass and building, progressive piano. Natasha's vocals are often absent, but this is a record that is undeniably smothered with her experience; her fingerprints dance over every beat and harmony. I am listening with my body, and my body is remembering its matrescence. When I listen, I am reminded of birthing my son. I feel the physicality of it in the bones and flesh that are now imprinted on the floor and I think about how we have grown, how much we still have to grow. I feel the heaviness of interrupted nights and muscle memory of feeding, half-asleep, in a darkened room, of his small body and my weary one finding a connection that has been made endlessly for millennia. This sound comes to me like time-travel and a dance beyond my control; it is a knowing, feeling thing. It has been so long since I have listened to music and known or listened and felt.

I think I had been ruling music out because it felt so far removed from what I had been through, from the sounds and silences that this seismic new stage of my life had offered up. But listening to *The Dream of Delphi* awakens a hunger in me I hadn't realised I'd been ignoring. Each track seems to end too quickly; I am suddenly voracious for more: more sound, more meaning, more connection, more listening. In the days after, I find music creeping back into my life. It is a tentative and shy little thing I am doing: plugging in headphones and listening to old Taylor Swift albums while I garden in the last of the evening sun. Catching earworms and singing them aloud. Putting on a record while I cook and acknowledging my senses react to it in the same way they do to the hiss of the vegetables softening in the pan or the clouds pinking through the window. I find myself longing for another layer to the soundtrack of the street I've come to appreciate over the past couple of years; not craving music to block out the planes overhead or the growing birdsong or the chatter of strangers on the bus and the polite, clipped tones of the recorded voice reciting Tube stations, but to add to it, to sit alongside in song. Music has changed in my life and I am only just beginning to understand what it could be, but it's there in a way it wasn't before. How good it sounds. How much I had missed it.

When I was in Natasha's living room, I told her how surprised I was to find the word 'midwives' on an album track listing; how it had seemed so radical. The music industry is not kind to mothers or motherhood, historically or now. In the 1970s, Stevie Nicks made a choice: 'If I had not had that abortion, I'm pretty sure there would have been no Fleetwood Mac,' she told the *Guardian* in 2020. Plenty of female musicians have spoken about how having children, to quote Lily Allen, 'totally ruined' their careers. Artists such as Beyoncé and Rihanna have used the industry's biggest platforms (the Super Bowl halftime performance; the Grammys) to announce their pregnancy, but among the adulation and celebration there is an undeniable sense among some fans that this will challenge, rather than enhance, their work. Rapper Cardi B was asked which she would choose – stay-at-home parenting or music – while pregnant (she responded, 'Why can't I have both?' then won the Grammy for Best Rap Album – the first female solo rapper to do so). Charlotte Adigéry signed a record contract on the same day she found out she was pregnant, a situation that she later said made her contemplate an abortion. 'I didn't think that the music industry would support it or even be interested in what I had to say after becoming a mother,' she told *Pitchfork*.

Two years later, she graced the cover of her breakout album *Topical Dancer* in a white bodysuit, a hole cut out for her expansive bump.

Other artists have channelled their experience into their work. U.S. Girls, for instance, created a warts-and-all funk track around the beat of her breast pump; Sharon Van Etten pleads with her son for forgiveness over her decision to work on an album called *We've Been Going About This All Wrong*. And female artists have ascended some of their highest career mountains as mothers. But the industry is still a hostile place to make creative work and raise children. Musicians' income is hugely reliant on touring, an activity that sits at odds with feeding, settling and raising children. Record label contracts rarely have clauses about parental leave, so many artists are left without a salary after childbirth. It takes longer to book in a tour or album-release schedule than it does to gestate a child, and mothering artists frequently speak of feeling a greater pressure to tour to prove to a youth-orientated industry that their career is not over. For artists like Margo Price, a country singer who sought wisdom from Loretta Lynn on balancing a working motherhood (Lynn told her: 'I just think you should have as many babies as you want'), touring took precedence over recovery from major abdominal surgery: she played a 20-show tour four weeks after having a C-section.

I tell Natasha I'm surprised to see the word 'midwives'

on an album track listing because, if I'm honest, I'm still questioning the general broader interest in art that prioritises the work of childbirth and mothering. For all its enormity, it feels like something that other people don't care to hear about or discuss. She offers a different perspective. 'Only in having Delphi have I spoken to lots of other women and realised how guarded or secret or shameful or difficult the conversations have been for some time. I wasn't prepared for that. No one had talked about it, which is fucked up. [Birth] is a rite of passage, it's a ritual, it's a mystical act and it should be treated that way. Motherhood is not a niche subject; it's universal to every single person in this planet regardless of gender. We all have a mother. I've luckily, quite naively, gone through this whole process being like "everyone's gonna love hearing about motherhood". Like, this is a radical act. I feel like I've been let into a secret. Everybody needs to know about this, about how profound and beautiful it is.'

After our conversation, as the magnolia flowers Natasha sings of in *The Dream of Delphi* bud, open and scatter on the pavements, I feel her words return to me insistently. I recognise the demands I'd put on my own postpartum body and mind, the rapidity with which society – so wrenched from the outside world that it others humankind from the rest of nature – expects women to return to the selves they were before giving birth. I'd subscribed to it; I'd been restless to leave the elasticated waistbands and small hours at home and return to the person I had been before I grew a child and helped him to leave my body. I hadn't yet learned how my very cells had changed with his creation, that I was never meant to have gone back to anything but only to move forward into new realms. I had not been given the space to make sense of it. I had not been given the quiet, and I had not sought it.

Still, it chased me. I heard it in the baby's breathing and his mewling cries. The quiet opened up between us in the nights and the daylight hours, it opened up between our bodies and it clouded and dulled and expanded my mind. It was a quiet that was daunting in its enormity. And that quiet was so accommodating it made noise itself sound different; it broke and bent my hearing, it turned my whole body into a means of listening. I wasn't listening consciously to 'nature' as much as to a whole that sounded different after a life-changing transition, one where threat and love and matter held their own new noise. Music had been absent in my life and at times it had never felt further away, but the quiet offered me the space and time to return to it. I learned to acknowledge the changes I had been through. I learned to understand how I was changing, how to navigate the new altered spaces of my body and my brain, to mourn the woman I had been before this and welcome the one I was becoming. And in the process, I was starting to fully listen again.

ERAS

The text comes through at 8 a.m.: *What is everyone wearing later?* I'm in the baby's room, picking things up from the floor. I take a photo in the mirror hanging on the wall and send it with a reply: *This, I guess?* I'm in jeans and a sleeveless polo shirt, an outfit of charity shop finds, constructed for ease and comfort and resilience towards small hands. Later, the 'later' being discussed in my palm, Taylor Swift will embark on the London leg of her Eras Tour. But before then there are friends to visit and birthdays to celebrate and little errands to run. I turn up at Wembley having been out since ten a.m., after passing my son over to his father in an entirely other part of London. It will take me several hours to discover the remnants of a raisin box in my back pocket.

Tickets for the Eras Tour — Swift's sixth global tour, her biggest, the one that made her a billionaire — went on sale a year earlier, days after our baby had been discharged from hospital after his illness. I had registered for them, but never got much further. Friends arranged trips across the continent to see it. I wasn't sleeping at the time. The baby's hands still wore the pockmarks of cannulation. It felt laughable that I'd be going to see a pop star, even if I'd loved her for years.

Swift's fans had been meticulously reporting the tour online. There was a tour film released in October, but I avoided all the coverage. I'd first reviewed Swift a decade earlier and had seen every tour she'd done since. I'd met her backstage and we'd spoken about her sexual assault trial, what it was to be heard and seen and believed. I don't know how many words I have written about her over the course of my career, but I suspect it could be in the tens of thousands. I knew I was absenting from something, not entirely intentionally, and I knew that it was more painful than I was allowing myself to realise. Online, I saw my friends go to the earlier shows and was shocked to find myself gnawing on the envy it induced. Not only for the gig – although I would have loved to have been there – but for the unadulterated fun and freedom it held; the hours spent on trains in the company of friends, the drinks before the show, the nights bunking down in cheap hotels. It was all so far removed from my life, which seemed largely to constitute laundering of small clothes, wiping of cheeks and fingers and going to bed early in a desperate attempt to catch up with my residual exhaustion.

I was asked to cover the Wembley show a week before it happened but I don't let myself believe it is possible until I am holding the ticket in my hand and standing with my friends in the crowd. Only then do I realise that I've been holding on to a nervous anxiety all day – that it wouldn't work out, that I'd be turned away at the box office or my husband would have to work late or the baby would fall ill. But I have made it, I am here, standing on the floor of a cavernous stadium, summer sky languid above me, the long catwalk of the stage mere metres away. I haven't been in a crowd like this, on the floor of a stadium like this, since my early twenties.

The Eras Tour is an unrivalled demonstration of pop superstardom: Swift, now in her mid-thirties and the most successful pop star of our time, conceived it as an exhibition of her professional musical evolution so far: 10 separate sections for 11 albums (she released another halfway through the tour), a bombastic reliving of her reinventions. A 3.5 hour, 40-song-set list demonstration of a girlhood, and then a womanhood, dedicated to song craft. The excitement around it had been mounting online for months, but now Swift was performing in London – until recently, her home for several years. This manifested on the streets: red dresses and finger-curl ringlets, the number '13' scrawled onto the backs of hands. As I walked to the stadium, I was confronted by how much I'd been ignorant of at the same time that I was reminded of how much I'd missed: the raw, ebullient glee of fandom; what it is to feel so seen by music that you will ape the person who made it, inhabit their trappings, paste their words onto your body. The air was fizzy with it, it was irresistible.

The friends I'd met on the stadium floor were also journalists, had seen the tour on earlier legs, were altogether bigger fans. But they were also all women I had emerged from girlhood with; we'd worked together on long newsroom shifts and got to know one another in pubs and at house parties. We'd cooked for one another and talked as the candles burned down. We'd stayed up all night at festivals together and bumped into one another in the park on blustery weekend mornings. We'd moved houses and danced at weddings. In recent years we'd met weekly at the lido, submerging our bodies into the water as the temperatures plummeted, feeling the endorphins flood our veins as our skin pinked. We started when the baby was a secret inside me, and kept going as my body pushed at the seams of my swimming costume. On the morning I didn't turn up, they knew it was because I'd had the baby. We'd all been girls who had gained guidance on how to grow up by listening to Swift's music.

Over the past few weeks, since listening to *The Dream of Delphi* and feeling something crack open inside me, I'd returned to Swift's work, along with music from other women I'd listened to earlier in my life – Joni Mitchell,

Sandy Denny, Little Mix, Haim, Robyn. I'd tend to the garden after the baby was asleep with Swift's albums in my ears, my brain catching up on the songs I thought I'd forgotten. I listened to her newest record and found it poignant that there was, once again, so much of my life mirrored back at me. Even after the year I'd had, even after feeling so removed from it all, Swift managed to capture that peculiar isolation of being in your mid-thirties and wondering how you felt so out of step with life, how everyone else seemed to have got it so right.

Swift's music acts like a form of time travel for me. Even without listening to it I can remember where I was when I felt that first connective tissue forming on the train home from the pub on a Friday night, woozy and sentimental with pints on no dinner and remembering what it was to be in the land of first adolescent crushes. Silly and indulgent and caterwauling with friends in the high-ceilinged living room of a house-share, knowing that this wasn't the music we might say we liked to people who didn't know us as well. In the flat I'd shared with the man who'd hastened my remove from music, alone and listening to 'Lover' for the first time as dawn spread itself across the city. Holding my sleeping son close to my chest, breathing in the smell of his downy newborn hair, humming the waltzing chorus and never wanting to let go. I can remember the dresses I wore and the bars we went to and the names that sat at the top of my text messages for all of her records. It's why it hurt so much when I realised I'd sleepwalked through Swift's latest era. It's why I hadn't let myself believe I'd been granted a reprieve to experience it.

The show is astonishing. Ambitious and expensive and heartfelt and camp; a glossy rattle through a life and a career that is hagiographic and knowing at the same time. And the same can be said of us watching – we've known Swift's work and her public persona long enough to know of its awkward moments; we love her anyway. This has been a long time coming. But for all the nostalgia and the invitation to reflect on what has been – people have pledged allegiance to their favourite Swift era in how they dress – the part of the show dedicated to Swift's newest material remains the most vivid and arresting. Her womanhood persists in being the most complicated and difficult part of the story.

A few years ago, Swift went on a well-publicised reclamation of her own back catalogue after her former record label refused to grant her ownership. In the process she released a new version of one of her most famous ballads, 'All Too Well', which was double the length of the original and shared new vulnerabilities about the heartbreak that inspired the song. Critics and fans unpicked the differences between the two versions of *Red*, the album it came from – the original, and 'Taylor's' – and commented on how similar her re-recordings were to those she had made nearly a decade before. But 'All Too Well (Taylor's Version)' is a different beast from the song we'd become familiar with. Swift's lyrics speak of a love affair that left her battle-scarred, and her voice carries that sense too: more raw, wiser, a stamp of maturity in its delicate rasp. She had been a girl when she'd been heartbroken by the subject of 'All Too Well' – barely 21 – and little older when she'd written a song about it. Now Swift had conjured something at an even further distance from her memories, and she sang it with more fondness and more fury. Wistful for the daftness of it all, a residual injustice for the pain that it had caused to her younger self.

From where we stand in Wembley, it is easier to watch Swift sing 'All Too Well (Taylor's Version)' than rely on the screens, her choreographic tics rippling through the memories we have banked from earlier tours at other times in our lives. But nobody has seen this layering of selves and perspectives played live before Eras – the song had been re-released during the five years that she'd been away from touring. A stage gimmick: as Swift sings about the New York winter, a gentle cascade of white confetti blows in from high up in the stadium. Snow, in June. It settles on my shoulders, on the bag resting at my hip, down my top. And as it does I feel myself let go, freshly sympathetic for the girl I'd been at university, whose older lover had also told her their crooked affair might have worked out had she not had the temerity to be so young.

Newly angry for every time I've had to make myself small and quiet and stoic at the expense of someone who should have known better.

People cry at Wembley and there is a soft pride to it — it's a sign of devotion to an artist, of engagement with the music. I am surprised to find that I do too, but I am also surprised by the catharsis Swift's performance offers up to me. I'd wanted to go because I love Swift's music and this is the greatest live show of it to date. But it also feels like a small miracle: that I've managed to be here, that I am able to stand here and relish it on its own terms, not with the cynicism of the jaded critic, or the adrenaline of the inexperienced reviewer trying to prove her worth; that my PTSD has been managed to the extent that I can go out and not envisage the baby waking up inconsolably. And as Swift performs her changing shades of girlhood and womanhood for us, I am surprised how confronted I am by mine, how I am able to plot them out: every heartbreak and love story and stumble and triumph and late night and lonely morning leading to the next. Perhaps it has all led to this, perhaps this was always how it was meant to be.

And I think we cry because we are listening together. It has been so rare for me to be surrounded by women I love, women I have grown up with, at a show like this. After years of going to gigs alone I had forgotten what it is to listen alongside others, as I had as a teenager —

those serious-seeming pilgrimages to local venues on rural buses and in the back of hard-won lifts. For nearly four hours we sing and laugh and scream and marvel at it all, shouting lyrics at one another and yelling them into the fading skies above. Just over a year ago I'd gone to see Beyoncé's *Renaissance* tour, stood in the Wall of Sound and tried to comprehend it as an observer severed from her newborn, pretending to feel normal. Now I am part of something – of my friends, of a fandom, of a crowd. I've managed to tune in. There we are, existing on our different planes of memory and nostalgia and womanhood, reclaiming our younger selves.

FRITH

THE CHANGE I FELT STANDING on the ground at Wembley wasn't immediate; I suppose they never are. Like any transition, these things begin before we're aware of them and take much longer to unfold than we expect. The long minutes of wakeful nights, the endless hours of wet afternoons, the rapid passing of seasons, through them all I had been changing how I had been listening. With time, with empathy, with patience, I had started to listen differently: compassionately at times. Embodied at others. It had made a kind of opening, a space for a new way to be.

I'd gone to Frith seeking quiet. Four hours and a ferry from Glasgow, on roads that became remote so rapidly we didn't pass a single supermarket. Winter's cloak was ravaged up here but still held in place, just about. The grey of England had shifted into deeper, brighter colours: the fiery russet of crisping bracken, the luminous green of moss and the pale stare of lichen, dripping from bare branches. When the sun came out it rebounded off heavy slate and wet rock and left them blinding.

We were staying in a cabin next to a sea loch that gently rose and fell with the hours of the day; reached it after miles of twisting single-lane road etched between hillside and water, its name painted next to a fence post. Inside hung photos of its construction: huge fallen trees piled on top of one another. The logs were a couple of feet across and dozens long. So heavy and thick that at night I was conscious I couldn't hear the baby as I usually could; a silence that was novel and uneasy. The logs gave way to huge picture windows of the loch, and we all found ourselves mesmerised by how the water moved. The baby would crawl over to the window and look out; whole hours seemed to pass in this way.

We were in need of a break. The winter had been long and hard; I felt the gnaw of it in my body and my bones. My head was so often both full and empty at the same time. We'd not seen the countryside for months, really. The baby had grown and grown easier with it; we were all sleeping more, I was only rarely summoned from my bed to tend to him overnight. I was on the cusp of feeling like I was able to breathe more deeply, as if I'd been underwater without realising.

We bundled up together in a small hotel room en route, eclipsed by fatigue. We learned that the baby chattered nonsense in his sleep, soft burbles in the dark. As we drove around Loch Lomond and through Glencoe I realised that I wasn't paralysed by the baby's discomfort in the car the way I had been in the summer before, veins still thick with adrenaline and the rest of me short on sleep. His cry had changed and I was able to process it as something else. It no longer acted as a tether to a dark ward corridor, listening out for the rise and fall of his screaming as a means of brutal survival. It no longer turned my body into a paralysing alarm or short-circuited my brain. I could listen beyond the panic and into understanding: he was tired and bored and protesting, and from behind the wheel all I could do was wait for him to settle. I took in the scenery instead.

I had brought my family on this trip because I had wanted to seek out silence. In tuning into the noise of my life I'd begun to realise how rare it was. Six seasons had passed since I'd gone to the anechoic chamber. I was gaining a grasp on the cacophony of my existence, of the noise I used to feel so overwhelmed by. I no longer felt as if I existed in a muffled bubble, bouncing along divergent waves of sound in a city constructed from clamour. I was beginning to identify and acknowledge the different layers of noise and sound for what they were: the rattle of a Tube train through its subterranean tunnel, the escaping hiss of a stranger's headphones, the rising melody of the steel can busker by the station. An ungainly but nevertheless valid kind of music.

But my life was still noisy, even more than it had been before. I usually woke to the sound of the baby crying, my body alert to it before my brain fully engaged. This started a sometimes 14-hour day of singing and talking in a one-sided conversation. I would send and receive voice notes, speak with colleagues or meet friends and, in between, spend hours at a desk to the tapping of a keyboard, the song sung by my tinnitus and the rumble of overhead planes, occasionally interrupted by a wailing siren. This was London, and she was loud. I wanted to know what silence sounded like now, if it had evolved from the strange, impossible absence I'd previously found. And so I'd taken us all away, to a Scottish peninsula only accessed by one road serving those who needed to get there, to try and find a kind of quietude I'd not encountered before.

Frith was quiet. The cabin was set down on the water, some distance from its neighbours. To push open the front door was to be subsumed into a space that was dark and hewn from the outdoors; another building made almost entirely from wood, like the Integratron. We filled it with our noise: the soft clatter of mugs on a worktop and the trundle of the toy truck the baby pushed along the slate floor. The opening of the wood burner door. The rush of peaty water through the shower. As this stilled, the cabin made its own sounds known. When the winds got up overnight it creaked and groaned, as if it were alive in its own way.

On the first morning we woke up there I swam in the loch. It was only later that I realised I hadn't listened as I nudged my body into the clear, salty water. Instead, I navigated the thrusts of seaweed and the shale underfoot, I felt the chill seep into my skin and calculated the depth of the water. Once I was in, I looked back at the cabin and the hills beyond, to the island caught out further towards the sea that I couldn't see from the shore. I'd not listened while I was swimming because I was still sinking into the sound. The more time we spent outdoors, the more I heard it. It felt like a magic trick, to slide open a door and reveal this orchestra: the tumbling waters of the burn that ran alongside the cabin, the rush of the wind, the calls of birds.

We went on walks in the woodland and along the shores nearby, and I recorded them as we did. Back in London later I would play these little snippets. They were poor recordings, just taken on my phone, but they captured the stillness of the place and our brief occupation of it. Alongside the rustle of our coats and the yapping of the baby, the recording caught our laboured breath as we climbed hills, the bustle of the wind against the microphone, the careful gravity of our footsteps in the wet undergrowth. Another recording: see-sawing birdsong and waves crashing and, again, footsteps, this time on what sounded like grit or wet sand. Another: water in transit, growing louder and tapering out; fewer footsteps. A bassline of something hard and churning.

I didn't label the recordings – I didn't need to because listening to them was transporting. They would place me back in time, in air that smelled of wet moss, behind glasses speckled with rain, my breath funnelling through my throat from moving my body, arms around a baby slung to my chest. The sound worked the same way as a photograph or a written memory might, a key that unlocked the rest of my senses. I'd gone to the cabin, to one of Scotland's most remote corners, in search of silence, to find out what lay beneath it. But I'd fallen for the noise. There was a quietude here of a human sort – barely any traffic, no planes, no voices aside from our own – but the landscape was a riot of sound so loud, so full-bodied I began to chase it. Getting caught in a rain shower halfway up a hill was its own kind of symphony. I'd stand outside in the mornings and close my eyes, wanting to situate myself in these long-lost noises.

In trying to learn how to listen better, I'd been drawn to a series of chambers. I'd not realised it at the time, but now they stacked up like notes scrawled onto an empty staff: the Integratron, the anechoic chamber, the birthing pool and operating table; the Outernet, the Wall of Sound, Hammersmith Apollo and hospital corridors. Phone lines and video recordings and headphones and giant architectural doughnuts shrouded in secrecy. And here the cabin offered another chamber. I'd travelled to the sound mirrors with an intention to occupy a unique space of listening, but in doing so I realised the oddity of making such a pilgrimage; to isolate one place of listening over another. All places held resonance: a sound system in the backstreets of Brixton, a deserted woodland on a Scottish peninsula, the distance between a bed and a cot.

Beyond Frith, looking back at the cabin from the waters of the loch, I recognised that listening happened when we understood where we were in our surroundings and how we occupied our bodies. That deep listening meant that the lines between sound and instinct began to blur. In the water I was listening as the seaweed tangled around my ankles and the soles of my feet felt for the jagged edges of rock. I was listening as the tide connected with the wind above. I was listening as I watched my husband carry my son out of the cabin and point to me, a poppy-seed-sized head in the water. I was listening as I noticed a balancing of my thoughts, a respite from the anxious barrage that had built up by stealth. Here, listening, I understood that mine was the body of a woman floating among it all.

EVOLUTION

When I stood outside Frith recording the burn that ran into the loch below the cabin, it was impossible not to think about Annea Lockwood, who has been recording rivers and water for most of her life. There, in Scotland, I asked myself if the burn sounded different in the morning to how it did in the evening. I would pull the car over to look at a rush of water by the side of the road. Maybe I was getting closer to inhabiting the sound; I certainly felt it surrounding me. Annea had told me that it had taken her until her eighties to arrive at a term for the listening practice she'd developed over her life. 'Listening *with*,' she had said, grinning. 'Suddenly that word "with" was catalytic for me. It did indeed articulate something I've been moving towards for a very long time and practising for a very long time, but without this trying to describe it.' Listening with the environment, listening with our bodies, listening with one another. 'It's no longer me as an observer and the environment out there performing for me,' she continued. 'It's listening with, that's a whole other comprehension of where we are.'

It's such a simple shift, from *to* to *with*, but it cracked so much open for me and created connective tissue in the process: to that Weyes Blood gig, when I realised I had been waiting for music to arrive for me, rather than give part of myself in a collaboration of listening with it. To the change Natasha underwent during the process of her matrescence that led to her creating an album about it – connecting with an energy beyond that which humans create, and waking up her listeners in the process. To standing on the boundary of inside and out, in the furthest reaches of Scotland, wrapped in the full force of sound made by non-human life.

Annea's work has often been communal: from the crowds gathering around the burning pianos to the invitation to 'do' the scores in *Women's Work*. But when Annea realised that she had been listening with, rather than listening to, it gave her something contained to share with others. 'It seems to make sense to other people also. The idea that gives me a tremendous amount of energy is that in thinking of ourselves as listening with other phenomena we are already shifting into not differentiating between ourselves and other phenomena. We are already shifting into non-separation. And non-separation brings caring.'

How much had I been separating? How much of this

was wrapped up in care? Since speaking with Natasha, I had been thinking of how we portion up these meaty parts of life, of her insistence on the vitality and radicalism of mothering, of its connection to much broader things. She made songs from her experience with an ambition to connect people to a world they felt distant from. When I heard them, I found a connection to something I hadn't realised I'd lost. Annea wanted to offer people a way of inhabiting the landscape we lived alongside as a means of connection; to listen with. These sounds are all of us, our bodies and the earth they rot down into, our blood and the water it is made of.

Seven months had passed since I'd watched the documentary about Pauline Oliveros's life and made initial requests to speak to IONE about it. I'd wanted to learn more about how womanhood and the company of other women had shaped Oliveros's work, and I'd hoped that IONE might be able to tell me. As the seasons shifted I tried various means of getting in touch, none of which worked. But then IONE appeared in my inbox.

Spring had turned. In some ways, I felt like a different woman from the one who had first contacted her. More solid, more centred, more conscious and balanced. I'd slept more, I'd listened more, I'd learned better how to understand the rewiring of my brain. But I was also conscious that my Deep Listening practice had not taken hold in the way I had anticipated after 'The Tuning Meditation' in the

Barbican cinema. I had not completed any sonic meditations. I had not turned up to the Deep Listening workshops that had happened in gallery spaces and pockets of open grassland in far-flung corners of the city. I'd not gone on a silent retreat or felt I'd read or listened to enough work made by Oliveros or IONE, who had co-founded what would become the Center for Deep Listening and whose work on dream awareness was crucial in developing the practice of '24-Hour Listening'. There was a formality to the Center for Deep Listening that reminded me of the expectations I had built up around my enjoyment of music: listen to the album, form an opinion, digest the back catalogue, go to the shows. I simply didn't feel qualified enough. When IONE didn't show for our scheduled video call, I figured I wasn't meant to find out more.

We do connect, in the end. IONE appears in large, tinted glasses and with honey-coloured wavy hair, emitting a rebellious glamour. Ours is the first of a string of meetings she will conduct that day, and during our call I hear emails and text messages fly in. It is difficult to square this business-like generosity with what I have learned so far – about the mountaintop retreats that birthed the concept of Deep Listening or the late-night dream workshops. IONE turned 87 days before we speak, a fact that astounds me – she continues to teach, continues to host film screenings and Q&As and celebrations of Oliveros's life. She seems 20 years younger. I have been struggling to know what to ask IONE: like Oliveros, she has made a lot of work, is still making a lot of work, and she's lived even more life. The concepts of Deep Listening are complicated and discursive, I am doubtful that we will even scratch the surface.

We speak about the early days, the ones in the mountains where there were no mobile phones or even musical instruments, when people stayed for several days, just listening. IONE tells me about how she and Pauline met – that, having moved in the same circles ('I was attracted to her name very, very strongly,' she says, 'before I even met her, when I heard people talking about her'), IONE invited Pauline to her birthday party in upstate New York. 'At the time, people didn't care about the country that much, you know, it was very exotic. Anyway, the car that people were wanting to borrow to come up to the party did not materialise. Nobody came.' But Oliveros did. 'First thing she did was go lie down. She fell asleep,' IONE laughs. 'But after, we sat outside and we were looking at each other, and there we told each other of a dream that we had – in the sense of manifesting. And it turned out that it was almost exactly the same: a vision of an organisation, this artistic network, worldwide, harmoniously and peacefully existing and creating and being connected. This was surprising to both of us.' It's something that IONE refers to as a 'recognition'. 'We were set up to look at each other. It really happened. It was extraordinary.'

That was the mid-Eighties. Forty years on and IONE continues to uphold that recognition even — if not more so — in the wake of Oliveros's death. I want to know how listening has changed for her over the course of her life; what does love do to listening, what does grief? Perhaps fittingly, she references Pauline when she answers. 'There was that term that she liked to express to others, "Let it evolve", she would say. "Don't let things stand still. Whatever it is, let it evolve." What we call change is actually evolution. So my listening is certainly evolving,' IONE explains. 'What I would say is that I am uniting with Pauline with her concept that listening has a real kinship with consciousness itself.'

Initially I am a little frustrated by this answer; I think I was hoping for a sense of easy tangibility: that perhaps IONE had listened, say, to something Pauline had made, or taken comfort in a kind of listening that had been supercharged after 50 years of practice. It takes me a while to understand what she is saying — that this answer isn't a fobbed-off vagary but a necessarily open-ended response, an answer from someone who is still learning to listen in new ways all the time.

When Oliveros was exploring experimental contemporary composition early in her career, IONE was looking into what happens when we take our dreams seriously, when we try to observe them and bring them into our waking lives — when we try to listen to them. Decades on, she's still doing that. If Oliveros argued that listening was connected to consciousness, IONE's theories of dreams being 'very close to the definitions of consciousness itself' run parallel to that. Oliveros may have died nearly a decade ago, but the two are still united through the work that bound them together as much as their marriage did. As IONE tells me: 'I'm enjoying that very much, expanding my consciousness.'

I am so aware of how much I want to ask IONE and how little time we have. How far I am along in this process and how far, really, I have to go. Part of me wishes we'd spoken months ago, another part of me feels woefully unqualified: I am no deep listener, I do not have 50 years of practice. What could I possibly have to ask someone who has? When I put my questions to IONE, she is warm and open, but the subjects are too big to manage in this way. It's too complicated, there's too much history that I haven't borne witness to, to simply say that Deep Listening was a product of Oliveros being surrounded by women after spending her academic years surrounded by men. 'Simply put, neither of us liked being "boxed into" categories. I'm speaking a bit for Pauline here, but we did talk about it,' IONE explains when I put this to her, 'but there's some uneasiness when you get pushed into these places and corners and people may have their own understandings and it may not be exactly what you mean. I never wanted to be called a feminist, for example.' Later, she noticed 'only women were coming to my workshops, and when a man did come, we couldn't go as far as we could otherwise'. It feels like a thread I want to pull, but IONE has another story to tell.

She mentions her son, whom she still works with – IONE had three children. Does motherhood change how people listen, I ask. She pauses, then lets out a high, unbridled laugh. 'Are you kidding?' She pauses for breath, then continues laughing. 'Oh gosh. What can I say?' She mentions a poem she wrote, part of which reads 'Mothers who are everything'. 'You know, I've really spent my life connecting to that concept, including having my own children. It's profound, and it's beautiful and it's awful and it's all those things. I wanted to experience it all, as a woman.' These feelings aren't unfamiliar to me. I think that's exactly why I find them challenging.

In the days after IONE and I speak, I realise how impossible a pedestal I'd put this conversation on before it happened. I'd been waiting so long to speak to IONE that I thought I'd receive a kind of deliverance, a neatly packaged-up nugget of an ever-changing philosophy that she has been developing for a lifetime. That I could ask her about women and sound and motherhood, get some answers, and have my feelings confirmed. Instead, IONE was lost for words; the questions I asked her were too – laughably, in some cases – enormous to answer over the course of just one conversation. I have not been on a Deep Listening retreat – my matrescence and my caregiving responsibilities have made such a thing impossible – and I have felt ashamed by how few of the sonic meditations in Oliveros's book I have undertaken. But I have begun to listen deeply; I have made recordings and I have felt my ears prick. I have felt sound with my body and I have been opening up to it; I have removed the hierarchy of sound I used to rely on as a register. I have been connecting.

Oliveros was such a huge part of IONE's life, and I was curious as to how grief had changed listening for IONE in her absence; but I struggled to ask her about it, we had so little time to talk and there were so many of her stories I wanted to hear. Still, IONE is keeping Oliveros alive in upholding her teaching and philosophy, in celebrating her birthday, in coming ever closer to the work she did. I'm sure IONE grieves, of course she does, but she is also constantly making connections to Oliveros's work; she's evolving with each reverberation that it makes. The word that stays with me after we speak is 'evolution'. IONE mentioned it a lot: the notion that nothing stays in a fixed state, that constant evolution is key to better understanding ourselves and the world we live among, how crucial it is for connection.

I have not been a mother long but already it has changed me. It changes me on a daily basis. For a long time, I was scared of that shift. I pushed it away; I was so desperate to hang on to the woman I was, to be unchanged by the enormity of growing a child and pushing it out and raising him into the world. I didn't want to be different, I didn't want to face the isolation it might bring. I didn't see it as an evolution or a development so much as an absence to be grieved. Music represented a part of my life that I had also felt was lost, and it felt lost because it was: realistically, I did not frequent dance floors or stadium gigs or festivals with the regularity I used to. But I have also never listened more deeply – to my friends, to my child, to myself. I had wanted clean answers, but IONE was offering something that I had to listen to: that I wasn't losing something so much as evolving. That I was changed because I had to be, because I have been through something extraordinary.

During our conversation, IONE asked me a question – a small one, about the garden she could see through the window behind me. It acted like a key that unlocked another level of connection. We returned to some of the things we had spoken about during the interview quite naturally.

'It seems like everything's getting more noisy,' I told her. 'I don't know if you find that?'

'Yeah,' she replied, 'people are trying to get through to other people, and so they think that's the way – to be louder. But that's not exactly the way.'

'What is the way?' I asked.

'Well, to listen to all of it. To listen to the loud and the soft simultaneously.'

The loud and the soft at the same time — a sonic meditation in itself. My girlhood was loud. My young womanhood was, too. I'd thought of my matrescence as soft, but perhaps it was the other way round. What is it to try and categorise these things? Is the roar of 125,000 people cheering in a field louder than the newborn breath that wakes you in the night? My body had become softer. My head had become louder. Whatever end of the spectrum they occupied, I had cleaved them apart and made them opposites. Here was a way of bringing them together.

DUSK

There are ten of us in total, the women who have gathered in a car park at 8 p.m. on a Friday night, and we're all strangers. I'm the last to arrive, apologetic and slightly haphazard, feeling conscious of the lack of binoculars strung around my neck and the silliness of the designer anorak I'm wearing: everyone else is older, everyone else is in fleece, everyone else's boots look sturdier. I am 120 miles from home. This is the longest I have been separated from my son. I am here for the same reason everybody else is: to listen to nightingales.

I have spent the past two days by myself in a treehouse in woodland a short drive away. It's a trip I made for space and solitude, although the anxiety I felt before I left almost made me cancel. There, raised twenty feet above the ground, I sit outside and listen to birdsong. I have downloaded an app that identifies the birds singing in real time and I am swiftly addicted to it, watching song thrushes and chiffchaffs and blackcaps and wrens and tree pipits and skylarks flash up in my palm as their chorus encircles me. In the morning, not long after dawn, I head out into the wetlands beyond and watch lapwings squeal in the air, beaks wide open. It takes all day for my boots and socks to dry out.

But it's the nightingales who have drawn me away from the city. They are something of an ornithological white whale: so revered in the books and the poems I've read, but I have never heard one – not even a recording. All I know about them is that their song has provided poets and writers and musicians with a muse for centuries and that they are vanishingly rare, besieged by the unpredictability of spring caused by the climate crisis, and the persistent devastation of their habitat – scrub and brush and coppice woodland, a habitat that was far more common before post-war agricultural industry wreaked havoc with ecosystems in the name of productivity. When I'm in the treehouse or the wetlands, listening to the birds, I hear my father's words on the walks we took across the fields as children. He'd point out the different birds and their songs. Since moving to London fifteen years ago I have become a glutton for birdsong – it is so often drowned out there. I lived next to the woods for a while, where they were loud enough to wake me up in the morning, but in general the dawn chorus is a rarer thing in the city. Blackbirds, wrens, tits and robins drift through the other noise. The occasional woodpecker. Sometimes we are treated to goldfinches and jays, but I couldn't tell you what they sound like. I don't know when or how I will teach my boy the names of birds' songs; it's harder to hear them in the city.

Our time in Scotland had been deeply restorative. We did so little and I listened so much. My PTSD treatment was coming to an end, and as winter shifted into spring I gained a balance that I hadn't managed for more than a year. I no longer felt as if I was lurching between giddy bliss or wild anxiety and malaise; instead I operated at a steadier rhythm, one that felt like contentment. One that felt quiet, in a good way. The baby turned one. The seasons repeated themselves. I pushed my body into new shapes and up against new boundaries and listened to it as it responded to movement. I realised I needed to make different pockets of time for myself. While I loved the city and I loved raising our son here, spending time outside it offered a kind of deep rest I couldn't manage at home.

We set off into the woods, led by Emily, part of the tiny team that manages the woodlands and keeps track of the birds who live here. She speaks softly and her hearing astounds me; every few paces she will pause and tilt her head, sometimes cupping her hand around an ear before pointing out what bird is making what noise and what other bird they are communicating with and where. She points out the sound of the water as it seeps deep into the ground beneath our feet. We are walking to the swell of the dusk chorus; above us the sky blooms pink from the sun setting on a golden spring day. Ripples and chirrups and echoes and calls soar into the sky in a beautiful cacophony. There are too many birds here for the app to compute and so we follow Emily and her assistant as they point things out, gradually translating what we are hearing. As we walk down a narrow path, flanked on each side by scrubby trees, Emily stops and gestures. 'That's a nightingale,' she mouths. We mimic her, pausing, passing the news to one another in whispers. The nightingale is singing alongside the thrushes and the blackbirds and the robins. His refrain is piercing and repetitive; it sounds almost pugnacious. This was not the call I had expected from all the mythology and romantic poems; the 'out-sobbing songs' that John Clare described. It is short-lived; like the nightingale Clare wrote of, ours also grinds to an abrupt halt, overtaken by an emulating thrush.

We've been given a taste and we want more. Three male nightingales have been heard in the woodlands we are walking – just three; 15 years ago there were 20 breeding pairs. Nightingales are migratory birds, leaving their sub-Saharan winter homes for the cooler woodlands of Northern Europe in April and May. The males go first and mark out territory. The females follow, flying in the safety of darkness. They are guided to their summer homes by the males' song; the birds that sing the best will lure down a mate. Once they have, they sing less; they will soon be occupied by little mouths. Emily's unsure if we'll hear much from them. 'For the past few weeks they've been singing their little hearts out,' she explains. 'But they've been harder to hear in the last couple of days.'

The skies darken and the chorus fades. The birds remind me of revellers drifting home from the pub: for a while a couple of stubborn ones keep popping up again. The quiet and the darkness descend both all at once and with a graduation that seems impossible to track. We pause increasingly often, standing in the woods as the skies close in. I am reminded of lying awake in my bed in the early hours, listening to the baby's cry dwindle as he settles himself to sleep. I feel his absence strongly; I feel it in my body, these 120 miles, these nights away. It feels heavy and it feels like freedom at the same time.

It's so dark now that only the yellow of the buttercups by our feet is really discernible. We all stand still, we barely trouble so much as our pockets. We are waiting, we are listening, we are being. I think of Fiona out in Svalbard, connected to her colleagues in a rehearsal of listening. I think of the invisible crowds I joined when I looked for the aurora above my back garden. I think of all the range of hearing and not hearing, of the phantom crying, of the noises that aren't written down but which frame women's existence for all of their waking hours. I think about whispers and what it is to be believed, of the belief that we are all holding in our still, listening bodies, primed for a sound many of us have never heard before. I think about the chorus that we make in our silence. I find it so poignant that we are all there, bound together with the same unspoken intention.

I don't know how long we have stood in this space. No birds have sung for a good while. Every few minutes a distant swoosh marks a car driving on the road beyond. 'I think we're going to have to drag ourselves away,' says Emily. We start making slow, careful steps along the slick path down the hill; silent disappointment hovers above us.

Then we hear it. An unmistakable sound. No need for Emily to point it out: it is unlike anything we have heard. A sound our bodies acknowledge before our brains have even a chance to register. A heart-soaring, gut-plummeting gasp of a noise, rising into the depth of the inky skies. High cheeps descending into trills and rising up again to repeat that insistent, compelling song. I feel my shoulders sink, my ribs tuck in with an exhale I didn't know I'd been holding. He sounds like an instrument, this bird, some kind of mythical wind instrument emerging from the trees. The song lands somewhere in my chest and unleashes a euphoria that reminds me of the satisfaction I used to feel when a dance track dropped on a club floor; my body enthralled to this release. Here we are, wrapped in sound. A kind of deliverance. When he stops singing we are hushed, then I hear one woman softly say: 'God, I've waited so long to hear that noise.'

Years, decades. A few minutes in a wood after dark to satisfy a curiosity we have all been harbouring. I record some of it on my phone and find it fitting that when I play it back later it could be any other kind of birdsong – this is a sound that needs context and belief and, perhaps, a communion of other listeners. I have found grounding with a handful of women I will never see again, listening to a noise I may never hear again, knowing I won't forget where it took me or what it showed me. Because while we stood waiting to hear a song from a nightingale we didn't know was there, I understood the value of the noise that normally filled my life. I felt I was swimming among a cacophony of reverberation, unable to engage with sound. I thought that silence might assist me, until I realised no such thing existed. I have tuned into the voices in my head that persist in telling me untruths, and in doing so I have managed to quieten them. My world hasn't become more sonorous or linguistic or musical or extraordinary; if anything, it has shrunk into the new realms of domestic hush that I once feared. But I have learned to accept these noises as the stuff of my life, just as I have come to accept that I am no longer the girl who lived her life through music. In her place has grown a woman, a woman who is tired and euphoric, a woman who has mothered and been broken by it, a woman who has come to listen and in the process learned that there are some sounds that will teach her about herself.

My life is a song, sometimes loud, sometimes soft. Sometimes discordant and sometimes made of nothing but perfect harmony. It reverberates through the people I love and the city I live in and the small hours of the night when I am awake while everyone else is sleeping. It will change and grow and I will change and grow with it. I know, now, that these evolutions will be difficult to navigate, but that they will be crucial. My life has changed, my body has changed, the woman I am has changed; and she will change again.

I drive back to the treehouse. Somewhere far off, a lone owl screeches into the night. I draw the curtains and boil the kettle, make tea and place it next to the bed. There, for a short while, I sit, my body alert to the sounds of this space. Listening.

The Last Sunday in May

I AM SURROUNDED BY NOISE. Tomorrow the country will be granted a day off, and it is making the most of it. The club on the corner churns out basslines and chatter; passing cars push through puddles made by showers, a slow, sticky simmer. White noise burbles from the room where the baby is sleeping. Somewhere, above it all, a bird is singing a song that nobody can hear.

I am tired. I have crossed the city today, walked tens of thousands of steps and carried my son and bought plants and seen my family and lain down, briefly, in the early evening sunshine on the lawn, to the umbrage of a questioning toddler. Soon I will take myself to bed.

Matt is playing music in the kitchen. It is a work thing, he is doing research. Snippets of songs blare out of his computer for half a minute and then stop. Some I recognise, some I do not. I lie on the sofa next door, too weary – or maybe too disengaged – to be annoyed by it.

After a little while I go inside. I take the bread from the cupboard and the good knife from the drawer and start carving neat slices for the toaster. A fraction of a song by Perfume Genius — an artist I loved some time ago now, an artist I interviewed in a hot chapel in Hackney ten years earlier, an artist I took Matt to see perform a gig I remember in snatches — soundtracks the soft clatter of pans being put away. The toast goes in, I lever it down with the familiar click. I have made a lot of toast since the baby has been born, more so than at any other point in my life. The music stills, Matt wants to play me a song.

Fat, shiny synths fill the kitchen over neat little guitar riffs. In the background, a snare snaps away. Male vocals gloss over the top, singing about tiny moves and twists of fate and watching the world shaking. Even at first listen, I can tell it's about love and loss and the bittersweetness that binds the two. Matt gets up from the chair where he's working, starts shimmying across the kitchen floor. He pauses at the sink, next to where I'm buttering toast, and he shakes his shoulders and nods his head, a little smile on his face. And then I'm dancing too; this is a song to dance to, it's a song that's impossible not to dance to, and we are both dancing, with a butter knife in a hand and that now-euphoric chorus and our heads thrown back as if we were outside, in the late spring rain, drinking it in.

In this moment, in these short minutes of noise and movement and jam and crumbs, my mind flashes through the scenes in my life that recall this happiness. The rise and fall of this sweet sound – of music – is offering connection to the deepest parts of me. I am in my best friend's draughty old student house with her and two of our school mates, drinking tea after a night out. I am in the kitchen of a house-share in Hackney, having cycled home from a club, listening to something mellow out of tinny little laptop speakers, not wanting to let the night finish, not quite yet. I am in a festival field, puffa jacket and bare legs, yelling into a midsummer sky that's only just started to dim, with tens of thousands of other people. I am in the snug little kitchen in Matt's old flat, sitting on the worktop in glittery shoes, eating peanut butter toast at three a.m. and singing between bites. I am sitting in a hospital bed, drinking over-brewed tea from a polystyrene cup, listening to an invisible newborn crying in the cubicle next door and watching my hours-old son startle in his sleep, caught somewhere between mother and not. I am dancing in a kitchen: one packed with friends, cigarette smoke floating out the window; one holding just the two of us, lit by candlelight; one on a dark winter's morning, dance music on the radio, Weetabix on the floor.

I feel these selves knitting together: the girl I once was, the woman she grew into, the mother I am becoming. I move my body and eat my toast and laugh at my husband and move my feet on the floor above the baby's room.

And as I do, I am not only listening to this new song, this jumble of melody and joy and sadness and rhythm and beat and feeling, but I am listening to myself. For the first time in a long time, I recognise her; I accept her. Not out, not next to a speaker or going to a party or gearing up for a twilight DJ set, but in love with sound on my own terms. Dancing in the kitchen like I always have. How good it feels.

FURTHER READING

Books

Rural Hours by Harriet Baker
Sound by Bella Bathurst
All the Beauty in the World by Patrick Bringley
On Listening edited by Angus Carlyle & Cathy Lane
The Sound Book by Trevor Cox
The Vast Extent by Lavinia Greenlaw
Birds as Individuals by Len Howard
Matrescence by Lucy Jones
Everybody Hertz by Richard Mainwaring
Beloved by Toni Morrison
Quantum Listening by Pauline Oliveros
Sonic Meditations by Pauline Oliveros
Deep Listening by Pauline Oliveros
A Musical Offering by Luis Sagasti
Hearing Happiness by Jaipreet Virdi

Articles and journals

Orgasmic Streaming Organic Gardening Electroculture, exhibition catalogue
'The Crying Baby' by Joyce Carol Oates, *New England Review and Bread Loaf Quarterly*, Vol. 12, No. 2, Winter 1989
'Dial-A-Dyke', *Trouble & Strife*, Issue 25, Winter 1992
'Gender Differences in Directional Brain Responses to Infant Hunger Cries' by Nicola De Pisapia et al., *Neuroreport*, February 2013
'Date Rape, "Sober Pills," and "Suffocating Control": Read Kesha's Lawsuit Against Dr. Luke', *Billboard*, October 2014
'Ryan Adams Dangled Success. Women Say They Paid a Price', *New York Times*, February 2019
'Do Babies Cry in Different Languages?' by Sophie Hardach, *New York Times*, April 2020
'Stevie Nicks on art, ageing and attraction: "Botox makes it look like you're in a satanic cult!"', *Guardian*, October 2020
'The disputed sound of the aurora borealis: sensing liminal noise during the First and Second International Polar Years, 1882–3 and 1932–3' by Fiona Amery, *The Royal Society Journal of the History of Science*, Vol. 6, Issue 1, March 2022
'The Science and Emotions of Lincoln Center's New

Sound' by Rivka Galchen, *The New Yorker*, October 2022

'The Invisible Work of Mothers in Music', *Pitchfork*, May 2023

Granta: Last Notes, No. 164, September 2023

'Diddy's violence left me broken, says Cassie', *BBC*, May 2024

Documentaries and videos

Deep Listening: The Story of Pauline Oliveros, 2023

God Turn Me Into a Flower (Official Video), Weyes Blood and Adam Curtis, October 2023

Christine Sun Kim in 'Friends & Strangers', Art21, October 2023

Podcasts

'Vibrators, Pauline Oliveros and Queering Sound: In conversation with Senem Pirler', *Girls Twiddling Knobs*, Episode 59, May 2022

'Jennifer Lucy Allan on Annea Lockwood', *Secret Admirers*, BBC Radio 3, January 2024

'Lily Allen and Miquita Oliver on fame, rock-bottom and the perils of being opinionated women', *Radio Times* podcast, March 2024

Albums

The Dream of Delphi by Bat for Lashes
Titanic Rising by Weyes Blood
Tapestry by Carole King

ACKNOWLEDGEMENTS

AT TIMES I BARELY REMEMBER writing this book; as with the shapeshifting, timeless days of early motherhood its emergence has blurred. What I do know, though, is that I wrote it during the hardest year of my life, and therefore my gratitude is not limited to those who helped with the writing of the book but also those who helped with holding me together beyond the desk. Thank you to Claire Bunyan, for your compassion and generosity in all ways; to Maya Thomas, for feeding us and bringing the right things; to Tilly Munro, for the phone calls in hospital and knowing what to say; to Kate McCann for cheese toasties and washing up; to Hannah Murphy for always checking in. To my fellow mothers: Anna, Heather, Mills, Ana and Gill, for the camaraderie and company in the long hours. I have been so thankful for your listening.

I am grateful to Rachel Mills, my agent, whose

enthusiasm for the genesis of *Hark* transformed it from something I was scared of into a book. To Helena Gonda, who balances clear-eyed editing and wild championing so well; I feel so lucky to work with you. Thank you to the team at Canongate who have birthed this book with so much care: Gabbie Chant, Rafi Romaya, Lucy Zhou, Jamie Norman and Claire Reiderman. Thank you to the grandmothers, Sue Vincent and Jane Trueman, who looked after the baby so that I could write and have bestowed us with wisdom and love besides. Thank you to the grandfathers, Matt Vincent and Peter Trueman, for taking the baby when life got too much to handle alone. To Shyrah Smith for watching him in those raw, broken afternoons and returning a spark of a writing practice to me. To Hannah Franklin-Wallis for the interview connections; to Camilla Greenwell for the adventure and the photographs; to Gabe Beckhurst for the loan of the books and to Jess Bailey for the introduction; to Anna Leszkiewicz for the Sylvia Plath knowledge; to Charlotte Runcie for the endless camaraderie. To Connie and Tom for Frith.

To Matt Trueman, who has held so much during the writing of this book and never given way; you have made all of this possible.